I found myself rejoicing as I re  *I could not stop reading it. It was too much fun. It is filled with inspiring stories, helpful anecdotes and necessary information. Dr. Gutierrez has done it again. He has given us a practical tool for high-level integrated medicine for the whole person.*

—Reverend Judith Elia

A manual for how to love your life! Dr. Gutierrez blends current science and good sense into a concise and engaging universal formula for improving your life at every level. Don't just take it home—take it to heart!

—Reverend Jon West

L.O.V.E.S. The Answer is an enjoyable, short book that opens the heart. Anyone can easily and immediately apply the messages to everyday life. The storytelling is like conversing with an old, wise friend who will have you laughing and feeling hopeful.

—Amanda Lies, PMHNP-BC

Nurturing us with long-forgotten wisdom, Dr. Gutierrez mixes in bright blazes of new insights and revitalizes us with his strong sense of spiritual prosperity. L.O.V.E.S. The Answer is a deeply delightful and heartfelt read brimming with fierce truths. Thank you, Dr. Gutierrez!

—Lin Silvan, Executive Director, Eugene Veg Education Network (EVEN)

Here is a sound life philosophy that is at once elegant and user friendly with its down-to-earth approach. It offers powerful motivation to carefully consider the life choices we make.

—Reverend Inge Tarantola

In L.O.V.E.S. the universal principles that are found in all major philosophies and religions, are shared in a clear and concise manner and is destined to inspire! Through the sharing of personal stories, wisdom sayings from master teachers, past and present, and the author's innate understanding of these principles the reader is masterfully guided into understanding how these principles will transform your life. When applied in daily life, these principles will promote peace of mind, optimum health, and an understanding of our purpose in, and oneness with all of life.

The profundity of this book opens the heart and mind to receive and experience at a deeper level, the importance of unconditional love and acceptance in our daily walk through life in this varied and beautiful world. Even the sharings of practical and helpful application of the principles is inspiring. Dr. Gutierrez has done it again. Well done.

—Reverend Sherry Lady

There is something for everyone in Dr. Gutierrez's brief yet thorough guide, that includes evidenced-based practices, for promoting wellness in mind, body, and spirit.
—Ericka Souders, PhD, LPC, NCC

Printed in the United States of America
Cover Design: Claire Flint Last

Luminare Press
438 Charnelton St., Suite 101
Eugene, OR 97401
www.luminarepress.com

Library of Congress: 2017940690
ISBN: 978-1-944733-26-1

L.O.V.E.S.
The Answer

FIVE PRINCIPLES
FOR INNER AND OUTER
TRANSFORMATION

Orestes Gutierrez, D.O.

LUMINARE PRESS

WWW.LUMINAREPRESS.COM

*I dedicate this book to my wife, Pamela,
and three children, Sofi, Maria Rose, and Boone
for their unyielding patience, support, and love
throughout the writing of this book.*

*For my mother, Maria, whose unconditional
love and support allowed me to chase my dreams and
realize that the sky's the limit.*

*Gratitude to the Unity ministers who have
inspired me to live my truth and write this book
on the Five Universal Principles. I would like to
recognize Reverend Jon West for his contributions
and Reverend Sherry Lady for her love and support.*

*Gratitude to Lin Silvan, Executive Director,
Eugene Veg Education Network (EVEN), for her
unyielding support for me as a speaker, physician, and
author over the past seven years in Eugene, Oregon.*

*A special thanks for my first Unity minister, Judi
Elia, for her enthusiasm, support, and contributions
to this book.*

CONTENTS

Stardust in Everyone

All You Need is L.O.V.E.S.

Reverend Judith Elia

I FOUND MYSELF CRYING, LAUGHING, CONTEMPLATing and rejoicing as I read this captivating book in one sitting. I could not stop reading it. It was too much fun. It is filled with inspiring stories, helpful anecdotes and necessary information. Dr. Gutierrez has done it again. He has given us a practical tool for high-level integrated medicine for the whole person. I especially like the acronym L.O.V.E.S.

When I was sixteen years old, I had a car accident. I went into a skid on a rainy day in Buffalo while driving on the New York State Freeway. My car collided with one driven by a drunk driver, my car flipped over a few times after I hit the guardrail and went careening down a hill.

I remember thinking, "This is how I am going to die." I noticed my body in the car from a bird's eye view and thought, "Judi is dead." Then I experienced a Life Review and saw my entire short life pass before my eyes. It was like a movie being rated on my capacity to love. I came back into my teenage body with the simple awareness that Life is eternal, Love never ends and Love is the only thing that really matters in Life.

Love. Love. Love. Love. Love. Love. To paraphrase the Beatles, "L.O.V.E.S. is all you need." Love is a synonym for the Tao that cannot be named, for basic Go(o)dness, the Stardust within. Practicing L.O.V.E.S. is a radical act that demonstrates compassionate action, self-restraint and intelligence, which conquer fear, lack of restraint and hatred. The sum of it leads to health and happiness. The source of true healing begins with each and every one of us. In the beginning we are born in Love and in the end we will return to Love and in the middle we get to practice L.O.V.E.S.

Introduction

ON DECEMBER 21, 2016, WHILE ON VACATION, I was pondering a title for my new book. After much deliberation, I decided on the title: *L.O.V.E.S. The Answer* and submitted my manuscript for pre-order. A myriad of possibilities exist when choosing a title for a book. I was left wondering, "Is this the right title for my book?" I did not wait long for an answer. Ultimately, the universe, in her own mysterious and most surprising ways, gave me the answer.... a resounding "Yes!"

The renowned psychiatrist, Carl Jung, defined synchronicity as events that unfold with no apparent causal relationship in the space-time continuum, yet they contain an invisible fabric of meaningful interconnection under the surface. In short, synchronicity can be defined as "meaningful coincidences." There are two explanations of synchronicity. A materialistic worldview sees it as random chaos of an unpredictable universe and attributes it to sheer luck. Whereas from a spiritual worldview, it is a cosmic dance, where the veil is lifted ever so slightly, to reveal a sacred message from the great beyond. As I was writing this book, a series of meaningful coincidences took place. Random events separated by twenty-two years, unfolded in a magical way.

The chain of events began over two decades ago when I was a teenager. During the Fall of 1995, I was a pre-medical student in college at Florida International University. To release stress from studying, I was singing and dancing to reggae in the dance halls of Miami. Buju Banton was my favorite artist. His now famous album *'Til Shiloh*, was released in the summer of 1995. Laboriously, I memorized organic chemistry jargon. However, I effortlessly committed to heart every song on that album. My favorite track was *'Til I'm Laid to Rest* which starts with the lyrics, "Strange, this feeling I'm feeling…"

Momentous events have transpired in my life since my college days in the dance halls. I am a husband, father, doctor, business owner, author, professor, and have moved to the Great Northwest. Twenty-two years have passed since I burst into song with Buju Banton.

On December 23, 2016, our Liberty of the Seas cruise ship stopped on the large, gorgeous island that Usain Bolt calls home. Despite my wife's best efforts to plan every waking moment of our vacation, it was a free day. Impulsively, the family decision was to sojourn at a world-renowned snorkeling spot. Jamaica has spots. Alas, Rockhouse and Ocho

Rios were too far away from port. Surprisingly, there was a special healing beach known as Doctor's Cave, made famous by an Osteopath! We were thrilled, especially after learning there was snorkeling there, too!

We were delayed disembarking from the ship and all frazzled. Coordinating the biorhythms of five people proved no easy task. Once we finally got to the taxi station, my kids said I look at home in the Caribbean since I am from Cuba. The native hostess reported an outrageous price for a trip to Doctor's Cave. Despite the price, we all jumped into the van. A special healing spot with renowned snorkeling was only 30 minutes away. We could hardly wait.

Yet, we sat in the van waiting and waiting...

We waited for 30 hot minutes in the "taxi." I mustered the courage and said, "Eh mon, how much longer be the wait, mon?" The driver reported the van could not leave with only five people. Unfortunately, we should find a small "taxi" to leave now. I summoned the remaining bodies out of the van and began a quest for a personal "taxi."

Another nice Jamaican man offered to take us to our special Doctor's Cave "right now but it will cost you more money." We changed our plans yet again... Inconceivable, how many times our plan vacillated. We were stranded at the Port of Falmouth, crushed by the thought we would never see Montego Bay, so close yet so far away...

At that instant, a charismatic, young Jamaican man drove by in a small taxi and said, "Wah gwaan wid yuh todeh?"

Since I am multilingual, born in the Caribbean and raised in Miami, I naturally responded, "Irie mon, weh yuh ah seh."

This driver offered to take us to a nice beach only 10 minutes away with free wifi and beach chairs. The cab fare and beach admission were reasonable. However, this beach did not offer world-class snorkeling or the majestic Dunn's River Falls. My disenchantment was transient.

Everything that transpired next is magical. Things happen for a reason.

I loaded my family into the taxi. After escaping the shiny gates of the Port of Falmouth, we encountered the real Jamaica with reggae music blasting in the distance. Then I asked the taxi driver, "When is Buju Banton getting out of prison?"

"Buju me brotha," stated the driver with a serious look on his face. He grinned. "He me brotha from anotha motha," he chuckled. Our driver sported a short sleeve white guayaberas shirt and tall head wrap concealing his dreadlocks. He wore a scraggly beard and was slim. Indeed, our personal taxi driver is Buju Banton's double. What happened next is eerie…

"Strange, this feeling I'm feeling, But Jah love we will always believe in, I know you may think my faith is in vain, 'Til Shiloh…" spontaneously our taxi driver burst into song. He serenaded us with one of my favorite songs from twenty-two years ago! Glancing back, he noticed we were vibin', swaying our heads in approbation. My daughter realized I was silently singing along. He sang my other favorite song, "While I'm Living, Thanks I'll Be Giving, To the Most High You know, I am living while I am living to the father I will pray…" and I got goosebumps as I lip-synced to his singing. He glanced back and smiled.

He dropped us off at Blue Waters Beach Club and it was epic. Live reggae music, comedy, tropical white sandy beach, warm water and sun bathing. We all forgot about the world-renowned snorkeling. Here is heaven on earth. This moment is what love feels like…

A few hours later, our taxi driver friend took us back to the cruise ship. My wife kindly asked him, "Please sing us one more song?"

Immediately, he responded, "May I sing you an original?"

What he shared with us is breathtaking! This complete stranger who lives 3,188 miles away from me, serenaded us with "Love's the answer! Love's the answer!" We were all stunned. My daughter captured a video of this moment on her iPhone.

In fact, my kids were unaware that just a few days ago I had submitted a book titled, *L.O.V.E.S.*

The Answer. When I informed my kids they were incredulous. They thought the sequence of events was surreal and magical. Indeed, synchronicity has the powerful magic of transformation with the Five Principles I live and share in this book.

Live Your Truth

One Presence and
One Power

Validation Through
Meditation

Experience is Created
By Thoughts

Stardust in Everyone

CHAPTER 1

The Magic of Transformation

I think that any time of great pain is a time of transformation, a fertile time to plant new seeds.
—Debbie Ford

"QUIT YOUR JOB NOW, PURSUE YOUR DREAMS, AND live a long and happy life. Otherwise, prepare for a premature death because stress is killing you, Hombre!" the pot-bellied Cuban doctor reprimanded Pedro.

Pedro is a rotund man, with a big red nose scarred by rosacea, and a gray mustache. He is an overworked, underpaid, frazzled truck driver. When his doctor gave him the diagnoses of high blood pressure, diabetes and obesity, he was in despair. Cheap rum became his medicine.

"I am killing myself slowly with a fork and the bottle," Pedro thought to himself. At only 57 years old, he had less than 5 years to live if he did not change his life! Pedro did not tell his wife Mary about his new diagnoses. He was afraid of what she and his three kids would think.

After five consecutive nights of blacking out on

the sofa from too much rum, Mary knew something was wrong. She could read him like a book. "What trouble have you got yourself into now?" griped Mary.

Pedro told his childhood sweetheart everything. His pain, his inner struggle, and his despair… "I hate my job and I hate my life," Pedro muttered.

"I know," Mary said. "I am here for you Pedro. Follow your heart," she softly whispered in his ear.

Pedro had a lifelong dream of being a magician. In his spare time, he practiced magic. He spent countless hours listening to audiobooks on magic tricks during his monotonous long hours of driving. Luckily, he earned enough money on the side as a magician to quit his day job as a truck driver.

Finally, he mustered the courage to quit driving trucks and became a full-time magician. Pedro the magician woke up every morning with a spring in his step and a sparkle in his eyes. Although he did not make as much money, he made enough to pay the bills. He was happy and living his life's purpose. When Pedro saw the joy on a child's face from a magic trick, his heart rejoiced. When an elderly man burst into laughter after being duped by a simple trick, Pedro was thrilled.

Through the happiness, wonder, laughter, surprise, awe and joy that magic engenders in everyone's heart, Pedro had found his life's meaning. Magic is universal. It connects all human beings.

Pedro, by living his truth, gained equanimity

of mind and was content. Sometimes money was tight. Although life still had its ups and downs as a professional magician, Pedro, Mary, and their three kids got by. Amazingly, even during challenging times, Pedro had an imperturbable mind. Through mindfulness and meditation, he discovered profound peace and serenity. For the first time in years, he was healthy.

"I love my job and I love my life," Pedro the magician thought with a gratitude.

The next decade flew by and Pedro was in perfect health. When he caught a sinus infection, he discovered that his Cuban doctor had died of a heart attack a few years back. "That is odd," Pedro thought. "He was younger than me." Pedro remained healthy, performing magic, and inspiring others for another 30 years.

Pedro the Magician, now 97 years old, was dying of a smoldering blood-borne cancer. The oncologist offered him weekly blood transfusions that might have extended his life another 18 months. "I've lived a long and happy life, Doctor," Pedro stated as he declined further treatment. With a full head of white hair and a large goatee, he appeared slim and healthy. A twinkle in his eye, the magician was lucid and playful until the end. He was in perfect health until the last 72 hours. Rumor has it the magician lost his mental faculties. The veracity of this allegation remains in question.

His wife, Mary, of 75 years was caring for him in the hospital for the arduous last couple of days. She needed a break and called the hospital chaplain for some relief so she could go home for a quick shower and nap. Mary wanted to come right back to be near her lifelong sweetheart, her first and only love. She and Pedro had been through a lot together...

"Please be with my husband for a while," Mary asked the chaplain as tears streamed down her face. "He is losing his faculties, I think he is hallucinating," she said.

The chaplain said, "Take care of yourself, Mary. Get your rest. Your husband has delirium or ICU psychosis, which is common. I'll make sure he is not alone."

The chaplain entered hospital room 108 in the ICU. It was quiet and dark. A full moon cast a dim light on the empty hospital bed. It was eerie, and the magician was not in his hospital bed... "Where can he be?" thought the chaplain.

"We have been waiting for you," uttered the magician from the corner of the darkened room. The chaplain looked around and saw only the magician. Realizing the situation, the chaplain went along with the magician's apparent hallucination. "We would like to initiate you into the ancient brotherhood of magicians," the dying old man stated with conviction.

The chaplain said, "O.K." and then gulped. What

the chaplain witnessed next is stuff of legends…

The nimble old magician hopped from one leg to another while chanting ancient incantations. "Amasuetepanete-saksutepenpanet-eaduanama-ketipajaru," over and over and over again. Suddenly, with dignity, the magician stopped chanting and slowly walked to the hospital bed and laid down in the mummy pose. Lying there motionless, he called the chaplain over to his bedside. The chaplain obliged. Pedro the Magician gestured to the chaplain with his hand, as he whispered, "Come closer." The chaplain came even closer. This request happened a few more times until the chaplain was so close to the magician he felt his warm breath on his face.

"Too close for comfort," the chaplain thought to himself. The chaplain was four inches away from the magician's face, staring into his luminous hazel eyes.

Then the magician whispered, "Watch me disappear!" At that instant, he closed his eyes and stopped breathing. Suddenly, poof—he was gone! His last magic trick.

Moments later, an ICU nurse entered the room and officially pronounced him dead. As rigor mortis set in, the chaplain looked at the corpse and was dumbfounded by the sequence of events.

In his last act, the old magician consciously shuffled off his mortal coil. Life was his stage, and for the final curtain, he put on a show. A magic trick only a true Grand Master could accomplish.

The chaplain had goosebumps, and a chill ran up his spine. The room was silent but emanated a sacred peace. This transition was the most peaceful and beautiful he ever witnessed. However, he was terrified to tell Mary that her husband of 75 years had died and she was not there by his side at the very end.

The chaplain called Mary, his voice trembling, and told her the entire story from beginning to end. Then he concluded by saying, "I am so sorry, Mary."

Mary said, "Don't be sorry. I am so happy you were there with him and not me!"

Baffled, he asked Mary, "Why?"

Mary said, "I know all of his magic tricks, and he never would have pulled that trick on me!"

Suddenly, the chaplain could not hold back his tears, when he realized the extraordinary connection Pedro and Mary had.

Some say the transformation from Pedro, the frazzled truck driver, to an enlightened magician, is an apocryphal story. We all have the power to live a long, happy and healthy life by practicing the five universal principles. Just like the magician, through the power of the five principles, we can experience an inner and outer transformation! There is magic in the transformative power of L.O.V.E.S.

First, one must discover life's purpose and live your truth.

CHAPTER 2

Are You Living Your Purpose? (dharma)

Who you are speaks so loudly I can't hear what you're saying.
—Ralph Waldo Emerson

DISCOVERING LIFE'S PURPOSE BRINGS SPONTANEOUS healing as we discovered in Pedro's story. Several amazing things happen when this occurs. Your mind and conscious desires, your ego and nervous system harmonize. Stress dissipates and you gain boundless energy. Magnanimous attributes such as fearlessness, defenselessness, bliss, and immunity from praise and blame shine through you. Timeless questions such as: Who are you? Where are your roots? Are your thoughts, words, and deeds lining up? Have you discovered your life's purpose or dharma? Are answered. Once you have found your life's purpose, you don't have to say a thing. As Emerson noted, the roots of your character speak so loudly, without uttering a single word. It is accomplished by living your truth. I am fascinated about the mechanics of how living your truth is related to health and disease. In fact, living your truth can promote a long, happy, and healthy life. Let us explore how.

My mission upon entering medical school, was not only to learn the best of Western Medicine, but to study Integrative Holistic Medicine on my personal time. During my self study, I discovered the most powerful phrase in all of medicine:

To know something is bad for you and to do it anyway is a CRIME AGAINST WISDOM.

How many people know smoking is bad for them but smoke anyway? How many people know exercising is good for them but do not exercise? How many people realize they have a sugar addiction but continue eating sugar anyway? The examples are endless.

What is a CRIME AGAINST WISDOM? The phrase dates back to ancient times. Here is the Sanskrit term and definition:

Prajnaparadha /praj·na·pa·ra·dha/ (pruj˝nah-pah-rah-thah´) [Sanskrit] in ayurveda, deliberate, willful indulgence in unhealthy practices that leads to unbalanced body functions and disease.

Let us delve deeper into this definition. How do we willfully indulge in unhealthy practices? First, we have to know something is unhealthy. For example, it's common knowledge that not exercising is unhealthy and that exercising is healthy. One definition of knowledge is that it must be true and you have to believe it. All of humanity and even children have common knowledge of exercise being healthy. With our current obesity epidemic, the natural question that follows is why are billions of humans on earth committing crimes against wisdom?

How do we overcome this difficulty of putting knowledge into practice?

The answer lies in a simple story about the Grand Master on living your truth, Mahatma Gandhi. There was a mother in India who had a 12-year-old son with a sugar addiction. No matter what wise words the mother used to discourage the boy's sugar addiction, she failed. Frustrated, the mother took a five hour trek, in the scorching sun, for the boy to hear from his idol, Gandhi.

Tired and exhausted after the trek the mother found Gandhi and said, "Oh, Great Soul, Mahatma Gandhi, tell this boy that processed sugar is bad for you and he should stop eating it."

Gandhi was pensive then replied, "Come back in three weeks."

The mother obliged. Then, three weeks later the mother took the arduous five hour journey in the scorching sun to meet Gandhi.

Gandhi looked at the boy and said, "Processed sugar is bad for you and you should stop eating it."

The mother, baffled and perplexed, asked Gandhi why he did not say this upon the first meeting.

Gandhi replied with a serene smile, "I was not qualified to advise the boy. Three weeks ago, I, too, was eating a lot of sugar."

There is a Universal Principle in this story that Mahatma Gandhi embodies: Live your truth since knowledge is not enough. Gandhi was a man of character as illustrated in this story. He walked the walk.

When you live your truth, you are standing firm and solidly on your own feet. You develop fearlessness, are stress free, and have self-worth. This engenders peace, equanimity, and promotes health.

When you live your truth, you stop committing crimes against wisdom.

One common reason that people commit crimes against wisdom is because of peer pressure. Yes, adults suffer from peer pressure, too, not just school aged children. Ask yourself, how many times have you done something just because everyone else was doing it and it was the easy thing to do? You knew it was bad for you but you rationalized that it was okay just this one time. The pastry for breakfast, the pizza during a lunch meeting, lasagna during the business dinner are a few examples.

Resolve to put your knowledge into practice. Once you believe something (vegetables are healthy) and recognize the truth (eating vegetables prevents disease) then you have knowledge. Put this knowledge into practice by eating primarily a diet that is organic whole-food plant-based. This same principle applies to daily exercise and stress reduction. Resolve to exercise every day for at least one hour. Resolve to improve brain health and reduce stress with a daily practice of formal meditation of at least 10 to 15 minutes.

Once you live your truth, words need not be spoken. Little needs to be said out loud. You will have peace and profound calm in knowing that your knowledge is being put to practice. When in the minority or in the face of criticism, you stand firmly in your truth. Society will pressure you to try a get-healthy-quick scheme such as Paleo, Atkins, Hard Body in 2 minutes, or Buns of Steel, but you will stand firmly in your truth. Whenever challenges arise, remember this powerful quote from Ralph Waldo Emerson, "Who you are speaks so loudly I can't hear what you are saying."

When you live your truth, you promote health, happiness, profound peace and boundless energy. Let me tell you a story about profound peace and boundless energy.

A Western journalist was baffled at Gandhi's boundless energy and asked, "Mr. Gandhi, you have been working fifteen hours a day for fifty years. Don't you think you should take a vacation?"

Gandhi smiled and replied, "I am always on vacation."

Gandhi was at peace, stress-free and doing his

life's work. Vacation is a state of mind. In fact, I was writing part of this book during a family vacation.

My wife asked, "Do you want to put away your computer, stop working and relax on vacation?"

I said, "I am having fun on vacation. Writing this book is not work. It is fun!"

When you live your truth, you not only put your knowledge into practice and avoid committing crimes against wisdom, you are stress-free and harness boundless energy. This behavior creates health, happiness, and profound peace.

There are several questions one should ask to know if you are living your truth:

> Is your mind telling you it is the right thing to do?
>
> Is this a selfless act, not pursued for reward?
>
> Is your nervous system calm and relaxed when you are engaged in your activity?
>
> Does this activity come easily to you?
>
> Are you having fun?
>
> Are you getting results?
>
> Are you excited?
>
> Are you enjoying the journey?
>
> Are you growing as a person?
>
> Are you being challenged?
>
> Are you being rewarded?
>
> Are you helping or inspiring others?

If you answered yes to most of these questions, you are living your life's purpose and are living your truth.

Living your truth also promotes exceptional longevity. However, longevity only relates to chronological age. There are other types of age that are more important.

CHAPTER 3

Delaying Biological Aging

How old would you be if you didn't know how old you are?
—Satchel Paige

IN MEDICAL SCHOOL, ALL PHYSICIANS ARE TRAINED
to look at a patient's general appearance and make a
statement on their chronological age. For example,
if I were seeing an 80-year-old who had a youthful appearance, and looks 65, the doctor may say,
"Patient looks younger than stated age." On the
other hand, if the doctor were seeing a 50-year-
old who appeared 65 years old, the doctor says,
"Patient looks older than stated age." Interestingly
enough, chronological age is the least important age.
Chronological age is nothing but a number, with a
clock serving as a dreaded reference point for the
inevitable: Getting older. However, aging need not
have a negative connotation if one accepts it as a
normal part of life.

In fact, there are four types of age: chronological,
biological, psychological, and societal ages. Briefly,
let us define each type of age. For chronological age,
reference a calendar for your birth year and add the

years until the present. Biological or physiological age is more complicated and there is no consensus on validated biomarkers for aging. Some use resting heart rate, blood pressure, flexibility, strength, coordination, endurance, questionnaires, etc., to determine one's age. A simple way to measure your biological age is by measuring your current VO2 max with a simple timed walk/run test. The amount of oxygen the heart and lungs can use during exercise is a measure of cardiopulmonary fitness (health of heart and lungs) and indirectly predicts biological age. One can then reference normative values for VO2 maximum based on gender and age since there is a linear decline in fitness of 1% per year after age 35. For example, chronologically I am 40 years old, but I am thrilled to report my VO2 maximum puts my biological age as an 18-year-old in excellent cardiopulmonary fitness! Psychological age is defined as how old one feels, acts, and behaves. Many scientists claim one's psychological age matters in predicting health, happiness, and longevity. Finally, societal age is the least important and relates to the expectation that society has on individuals based on current chronological age. For example, in American society, in the late teens you're in college, then 20s and 30s you work and have a family, retire at 65, then you're a grandparent, etc. This is also known as the "social clock" or a set of norms and expectations that the culture you live in place upon you based on your current chronological age.

How can we stay young at heart? One secret lies in the stories of those with exceptional longevity. For instance, one of the oldest female WWII veterans, Alyce Dixon, while celebrating her 108th birthday, was recently quoted as saying, "God has been so good. He left me here with all these lovely people and all these nice things they're saying. I hope they mean it." Ms. Dixon even visited the White House and told the Obamas jokes in the oval office! Nursing assistant Mary Matthews said, "Oh yeah, she's a real jokester. She likes to tell jokes."

According to Mayo Clinic, laughter is a great form of stress management. It can release endorphins, stimulate the relaxation response, decrease muscle tension, improve immune function, relieve pain, increase personal satisfaction, and improve mood. Perhaps we could add that humor promotes longevity? Indeed, many centenarians are known for their jokes. Jean Clement, who is the longest lived human in recorded history at 122, was fond of saying, "I have only had one wrinkle my whole life, and I'm sitting on it!"

In my professional career as a doctor, I have seen many patients with exceptional longevity. It is no coincidence that they had a great sense of humor. One afternoon in Mayo Clinic, a 101-year-old centenarian came in for a Mini Mental Status Exam (MMSE). The MMSE is thirty questions to assess for dementia or mild cognitive impairment.

The first thing she said was, "Doctor, I like a good joke!"

I replied "Oh, really? Tell me a joke."

I thought to myself, "If she can tell me a joke, she is lucid and would likely pass the MMSE since one of the first things to go with cognitive decline is a sense of humor." I put down my pen and paper she told me this joke:

"There was a nine-year-old boy who was walking to church on Sunday morning. As he approached the front lawn of the church, he saw a big picture with little American flags all around the border of the picture frame. Inside the frame, there were handsome men in uniform. As the young boy stared at the picture, the minister walked up to him.

'Young boy, those are all the men who died in service.'

The boy looked at the minister and asked, 'The 9 o'clock service or the 11 o'clock service?'"

After the 101-year-old told me this story she had passed the MMSE.

The anecdotal stories from centenarians are good reminders that a way to reduce stress and tap into the relaxation response is through humor and laughter. A positive psychology, staying young at heart with a youthful vigor promotes a healthy biological age. Your mythology becomes your psychology which manifests as your biology. How you think and feel create your belief system which influences every cell in your body.

However, living your truth is not about living to 100 years old. It is about the acquisition of wisdom that comes from inner knowledge of the self.

CHAPTER 4

Yoga of Knowledge (jnana)

The fool doth think he is wise, but the wise man knows himself to be a fool.
—William Shakespeare

EVEN IF ONE DOES EVERYTHING RIGHT, WITH proper nutrition, exercise, stress reduction, social support and even humor, death is inevitable. Father Time is undefeated. However, we live in a culture that worships immortality as if plastic surgery will allow us to live forever. It is a crime against wisdom, *prajnaparadha*. Specifically, to know we all will someday die but to act as if one will live forever is ignorance.

A student once asked the great sage Yudhisthira, "What is the most surprising thing?"

Sage Yudhisthira responded, "The most surprising thing is that even though every day one sees countless living entities dying, he still acts and thinks as if he will live forever."

The wisdom of knowing and embracing our mortality brings about freedom. There is a famous parable about the Buddha regarding this matter.

A mother's four-year-old son died tragically. She brought the boy's dead body to the Buddha so he might bring him back to life. The mother was grieving uncontrollably and in the depths of despair. The Buddha, with great compassion, gave a subtle teaching. He instructed the grieving mother to bring a mustard seed for every household that has not been touched by death. The mother frantically knocked on hundreds and hundreds of doors, desperately searching for one household that had been spared from the clutches of death. In every house, there was a friend, brother, sister, mother, father, uncle, aunt, cousin, neighbor, or pet that had died. The grieving mother returned to the Buddha, bowed at his feet, and became his disciple.

Yoga of Knowledge (Jnana) is not a knowledge about material things or knowing a lot. It is a form of experiential knowledge which gives release from bondage. In the Star Wars movie, *Rogue One*, there was a line by a wise sage, as he was addressing a restless individual, "There are many forms of prison and you seem to carry yours wherever you go." Jnana yoga releases one from the metaphorical prison of attachment to materialism. It is knowing we are mortal and being comfortable in our own skin. It is self-knowledge. As Socrates famously said, "Know thyself." Also, in Jnana Yoga one remains humble in pursuit of wisdom and knows his or her human limitations.

One simple but profound practice of wisdom is contemplating the Five Remembrances every day. This teaching comes from the *Upajjhatthana Sutta*. The English translation from the original text on the Five Remembrances:

I am sure to become old; I cannot avoid aging.

I am sure to become ill; I cannot avoid illness.

I am sure to die; I cannot avoid death.

I must be separated from all my belongings, including my friends, family, possessions, name, fame, etc.

I am the owner of my actions; my actions are my only true belongings.

The Five Remembrances acknowledge the fragility and ultimate mortality of all humans. This is difficult to do in our materialistic society. When my youngest child was only 12 years old, he asked me about immortality. He wanted to know if it was possible for humans to live forever. After discussing the pros and cons of immortality my youngest son said, "I don't want to be immortal. I want to grow old and die." This took a lot of courage, insight and wisdom. New research suggests that wisdom is not a product of older chronological age. Wisdom is a product of good judgement and attainable at any age. We have all met the 55-year-old who acts like a 12-year-old. Similarly, there are young adults wise beyond their years.

There is a dichotomy between inner knowledge of the self, and outer knowledge of materialistic things, that parallels the paradigms of East and West. This dichotomy is reflected in the Western materialistic worldview and Eastern spiritual traditions. For instance, in American society it is admirable to accumulate lots of knowledge about things and even know intricate details about other people's lives. Lao Tzu said, "It is wisdom to know others; It is enlightenment to know one's self."

This lack of self-knowledge can lead to The Dunning-Kruger Effect. It is not knowing how much you really don't know. Another way of saying it is your perceived competence is inversely proportional to your actual competence (the more you think you know, the less you know). As Socrates famously said, "The only thing I know is that I know nothing."

On the contrary, when cartoon character Homer Simpson goes out on his adventures, supremely confident in his abilities, we recognize his incompetence. His ignorance is laughable. It is laughable and ignorant how American culture worships immortality and does not recognize the Eastern wisdom on death and dying. In the East, death is viewed as a creative transformation and is not something to be feared. From a relative point of view there is birth and death on the material plain of existence. However, from an absolute point of view, birth and death are illusory, a cosmic dance of hide and seek. For example, the appearance (birth) and disappearance (death) of a wave are a form of relative existence. From an absolute point of view, the waves are the vast ocean, and there is no birth or death of a wave. On the relative plane of existence there is a law of cause and effect and there appears to be birth and death. Wisdom tells us that birth and death are illusory and are outside our conscious control. Self-knowledge is to know our physical bodies are subject to the laws of causes and effect and have a relative existence. However, the energy of consciousness which some call the soul has an absolute existence and survives the death of the physical body.

In the Gita, there is a verse about the absolute existence of the soul:

> *As a person discarding worn-out clothes, puts on new garments, likewise the embodied soul, casting off worn-out bodies, enters into other bodies which are new.*

—Bhagavad Gita, Ch 2 v 22

In the material plane that is governed by the law of cause and effect, one has to shed their clothes, sometimes even before they are "worn out."

One of Buddha's most loyal disciples, Ananda, was sent to give a guided meditation to a dying man. This dying man was Anathapindika, a great benefactor who was a common householder. Anathapindika was actively dying. Ananda went through a meditation practice on the illusory nature of the physical world. Ananda started by saying, "This body is not me. I am not caught in this body, I am life without boundaries and life without limits." He repeated the same meditation with every body part, these eyes, these ears, this tongue, this mind, etc. When the monk finished with this profound meditation exercise, Anathapindika cried. He had served the Buddha for 35 years and this was the first time he had heard this teaching. Ananda said, "What is wrong? Are you in pain?"

Anathapindika replied, "No, I am not in pain. I am crying because I finally understand this great teaching and it is so beautiful."

Ananda explained, "Dear Friend, we monks practice this teaching every day."

The householder implored, "Please tell the Buddha that the lay people should practice this profound teaching as well and not wait until they are on their deathbed."

This teaching is now practiced by both lay practitioners and monks. Thich Nhat Hanh recommends this poem be sung to a dying person so they can transition peacefully and without fear.

This body is not me.
I am not limited by this body.
I am life without boundaries.

I have never been born,
and I have never died.

Look at the ocean and the sky filled with stars,
manifestations from my wondrous true mind.
Since before time, I have been free.

Birth and death are only doors through which we
     pass,
sacred thresholds on our journey.
Birth and death are a game of hide-and-seek.

Eventually, no matter how much we practice we will have to shed our worn out bodies.

The following story illustrates the law of cause and effect in a humorous way.

The Grim Reaper visits everyone but we never know when he will come. The Shadow of Death knocked on the door of a sixty-four-year old man. The man opened the door and turned pale. Before him stood the shadow of death. The man begged the Grim Reaper for just one year to get all of his affairs in order and complete all the things on his bucket list. He was planning to retire at 65 and really have fun. The Grim Reaper felt a little compassion and granted him one year but promised to collect him when his time was up. Then at one year, he realized that he had not accomplished all he wanted to accomplish and his life was not fulfilled. He hid from the Grim Reaper. He shaved his head, went to a bar and got drunk, and laid down in a corner.

The man thought to himself, "The Grim Reaper will never find me here."

Then The Grim Reaper, after a long day searching for him, was tired and frustrated. He went to the bar to have a drink. He told the bartender although he could not find the person he was looking for, he still needed to take one soul back to the underworld with him. The Grim Reaper announced, "I'll take that bald drunk guy in the corner!" This story illustrates the unpredictability of death. We should cherish and live each day as if it were our last.

Wisdom is knowing we all die and we don't know when it will happen. Fear of death is bondage. One form of wisdom is attaining fearlessness, known as abhaya in Sanskrit. There are five kleshas, or poisons, in the Vedantic tradition that lead to bondage. These five poisons are ignorance, egoism, attachment, hatred, and fear of death. The remedy is attaining wisdom through knowledge of the self, defenselessness by not taking anything personally, inner detachment, love, and fearlessness. Harnessing these five qualities leads to freedom from bondage. Fearlessness is a quality that is expressed in this Native American poem from an unknown author:

> *Don't stand by my grave and weep*
> *For I am not there, I do not sleep*
> *I am a thousand winds that blow*
> *I am the diamond's glint on snow*
> *I am the sunlight on ripened grain*

I am the gentle autumn's rain
When you awaken in morning's hush
I am the swift uplifting rush
Of quiet birds in circle flight
I am the soft stars that shine at night
Do not stand at my grave and cry
I am not there, I did not die.

Another attribute that develops when you you live your truth is equanimity. With equanimity there is self-control and a quiet mind develops. Think of equanimity as an imperturbable mind. This quality of mind promotes optimal health. It will surely allow one to obtain inner freedom. Here is a powerful story that highlights equanimity.

In ancient times there was a samurai whose sacred duty was to be an executioner. He would behead convicted criminals who had committed heinous crimes such as rape and murder. One day the samurai was getting ready to execute a murderer who was condemned to death. He took out his sword from its sheath and moments before he was to strike the neck, the murderer spat in the samurai's face. Paradoxically, the samurai put his sword back into his sheath and walked away. Then a younger samurai, asked him why he had not beheaded the heinous murderer who had just spat in his face. The younger samurai thought that would have given him all the more reason to execute the criminal since he had just disrespected him. However, what the elder samurai said was instrumental to the teaching.

The wise samurai said, "When the criminal spat in my face, I became angry and lost my inner emotional control." He could not perform his sacred duty as a samurai with any trace of anger in his body. The secret code of the samurai was to do his sacred duty with complete and utter detachment and equanimity. Once he had lost his poise, he was no longer in control and could not perform his duty well.

Wisdom is gaining self-knowledge and being able to witness thoughts and emotions without reacting. With practicing Jnana Yoga one attains inner freedom and equanimity no matter what turbulent situation is in our life. Self-knowledge allows us to face the five poisons, especially the fear of death. The remedy for the five poisons is attaining wisdom through knowledge of the self, defenselessness by not taking anything personally, inner detachment, love, and fearlessness.

Discovering your life's purpose and living your truth is wisdom and is health promoting. When you put your knowledge into practice and avoid committing crimes against wisdom, you are stress-free and harness boundless energy. This creates health, happiness, and profound peace. Ask yourself these questions frequently to know if you are living your truth:

Is your mind telling you it is the right thing to do?

Is your ego not involved and you're not pursuing a reward?

Is your nervous system calm and relaxed when thinking of your project?

Does this activity come easily to you?

Are you having fun?

Are you getting results?

Are you enjoying the journey?

Are you growing?

Are you challenged?

Are you rewarded?

Are you helping or inspiring others?

If you answered "yes" to most of these questions, you are living your life's purpose and are living your truth. Living your truth also promotes health, exceptional longevity, and delays biological aging.

Live Your Truth

One Presence and
One Power

Validation Through
Meditation

Experience is Created
By Thoughts

Stardust in Everyone

CHAPTER 5

The Power Of Silence

The language of God is Silence. Everything else is a poor translation.
—Thomas Keating

IN TODAY'S SOCIETY PEOPLE ARE ADDICTED TO empty chatter. The normal thing is to fill one's time with trivial conversation and noise. Many people feel that a car trip, elevator ride, or dinner party must be filled with empty talk. However, silence should not be viewed with a negative connotation. In fact, many traditions honor silence for bringing healing and rest.

Mahatma Gandhi once said, "Speak only if it improves upon silence."

This is an apt quote for our times of offensive and rude commentary and frivolous chatter. Conversations are not the problem. We need to have a healthy period of silence in between thoughtful speech, like the space between notes, to hear the music of our words when we speak.

Eleanor Roosevelt once said, "Great minds discuss ideas; average minds discuss events; small minds discuss people."

When one's mind is not filled with gossip about people, a vacuum is created that allows the nourishing and healing presence of silence to enter. With silence our minds become more quiet and peaceful. Also, our minds become a fertile ground for the perception of truth. Silence engenders fecundity *fruitful* of mind.

Unity co-founder Charles Fillmore was inspired by the healing power of silence. He started a personal spiritual practice of honoring silence every day as a way of gaining self-knowledge and truths. Instead of reading about the divine, he wanted to have first-hand experience. Charles Fillmore said, "If I am Spirit, and this God they talk so much about is Spirit, we can somehow communicate, or the whole thing is a fraud."

He took it upon himself to commune with God every day by practicing silent meditation. Charles and his wife, Myrtle, both had transformative healing experiences through the power of silence. In the late 1880's, they founded Silent Unity. That ministry has been a continuous prayer hotline ever since. A trained prayer minister responds to a prayer request by phone, email, letter, or mobile app and prays for the individual for thirty days. At Silent Unity, anyone can reach out for a prayer request irrespective of their religion, race, or gender.

There was a great debate over the truth of the

Universe between a Yogi who was a Vedanta scholar and a fundamentalist from the Christian tradition. They went back and forth between the existence of God and delved deeply into evolution and consciousness.

The Christian fundamentalist said to the Yogi, "The more I hear you speak, the more I believe you are an atheist!"

The Yogi replied, "I used to be an atheist until I realized I was God."

The fundamentalist then angrily said, "Are you denying the divinity of Jesus?"

The Yogi said, "Oh, heavens, no, I would not deny the divinity of anyone!"

At this the fundamentalist got even more furious. No matter what religion you practice, living your truth is about discovering universal truths from within. There is no dogma in this approach to self-discovery.

Unity grew out of the New Thought movement. Its predecessors, the Transcendentalists, were also deeply reliant on discovering self-knowledge and tapping into the power of silence. Henry David Thoreau and Ralph Waldo Emerson were two of America's prominent transcendentalists in the 1830s. In fact, Thoreau was inspired by Emerson and wrote the classic book, Walden, during two years of self-reflection in a log cabin in the wilderness, while living on Emerson's property. Thoreau spent many days and nights in solitude. However, he did not feel alone because he formed a deep connection with all of nature. Spending even one day in silence is virtually impossible for most people today. Remarkably, Thoreau spent two years in a log cabin in the wilderness and was completely self-sufficient and regularly immersed in solitude. He lived in a time that revered silence and self-reliance as something sacred.

In the book, *Embracing Truth In Times of Adversity*, there is a wonderful story told about Ralph Waldo Emerson. It is said Emerson had a long term friendship with Thomas Carlyle and they communicated via letters for years. When Emerson finally visited Europe, he made a special trip to Scotland to visit Carlyle. Carlyle greeted Emerson warmly, and they each lit a pipe. The first night they finally met face to face, they sat together in silence without a single word being uttered. It is described as being an ecstatic experience for both of them, to finally be in each other's presence without uttering a single word. This story may sound apocryphal, but to them silence was sacred. They valued the inner world more than external trappings. Two great thinkers meeting face to face for the first time did not have time for trivial chatter. Let us embrace the power of silence as an everyday habit.

Elizabeth Kubler Roth states it well:

Learn to get in touch with the silence within yourself, and know that everything in life has purpose. There are no mistakes, no coincidences, all events are blessings given to us to learn from.

CHAPTER 6

The Power of Nonviolence (ahimsa)

At the center of nonviolence stands the principle of love.
—Martin Luther King, Jr.

NEGATIVE THOUGHTS MANIFEST IN OUR BODIES AS stress hormones, muscle spasms, elevated heart rate, elevated blood pressure, premature aging, anxiety, and depression. Persistent negative thinking is violence. Through the intimate mind-body connection persistent negative thoughts manifest in our bodies. Nonviolence or ahimsa is an ancient practice that involves not only physical action but also the movement of thoughts. An ancient Chinese proverb articulates this point:

Be careful of your thoughts, for your thoughts become your words.

Be careful of your words, for your words become your actions.

Be careful of your actions, for your actions become your habits.

> *Be careful of your habits, for your habits become your character.*
>
> *Be careful of your character, for your character becomes your destiny.*

I would add:

> *Be careful of your emotions, for your emotions can become countless restless thoughts.*

Emotional turbulence can lead to a myriad of negative and violent thoughts. In practicing ahimsa or nonviolence, we must be careful of our thoughts, emotions, and behavior. If our thoughts are negative, pessimistic, hypercritical, sarcastic, derogatory, angry, racist, bigoted, homophobic, Islamophobic, etcetera, we must pay attention and be careful with these thoughts as they arise. There is a specific mindfulness technique that can eradicate violent thoughts. In Eastern wisdom traditions, it is known as the silent witness. In modern psychology, it is called metacognitive awareness also known as "thinking about thinking." This mindfulness technique can also apply to our feelings and emotions. We will explore techniques in a later chapter in this book.

How does ahimsa apply in daily life? Through dialectics we can see that killing animals for food is a violent action if there are other alternative healthy food sources available. This reasoning will not apply to someone with scarce food resources living in the wild. Most people living in the developed world can sustain themselves with healthy whole-foods plant-based diet. In fact, many spiritual traditions have recommended such a diet to engender a peaceful mind and healthy body. Just because we have not seen factory farming, slaughterhouses, and the violence in killing animals for food, does not make us immune from directly and indirectly paying for the consequences. The price we pay is chronic disease and stress on the human body by consumption of animal foods. Our earth pays the price through deforestation and the destructive effects on climate change.

Ahimsa is a process that leads to deep inquiry or reflection. It is the process of questioning, investigating, and analyzing the material world around you to find out the truth. We should live our lives in a non-violent way with fearlessness and pure love. Why shouldn't we apply the same principle of ahimsa to the food we consume? In fact, we should be very diligent to inquire every time we put food in our mouths and ask, "Where did this food come from?" If we apply this principle, and deeply look into where our food is coming from, we will choose local organic plant-based food as the only safe food for human consumption.

The precautionary principle states that when choosing between competing hypotheses, always choose the safe action. As an example, when choosing between an animal food, say a piece of meat such as salmon, there is the risk of exposure to mercury, polychlorinated biphenyl, and dioxins versus a piece of safe organic broccoli. I would say choosing the organic plant-based food is 100% safe because we know for a fact that eating this food is not harmful for your body. Since we have the choice, shouldn't we consume only the foods that we know are 100% safe for us? Therefore, plant-based food is what you should consume. When looking at the scientific literature on nutrition, it is easy to cherry pick an article and massage the information to suit your needs. There may be articles stating that saturated fat is good for you. One may find articles, usually industry sponsored, that eating animal foods such as lean meats, butter, and eggs are healthy. However, there is also an abundance of scientific literature stating the opposite. In this setting when there are competing views on what is the optimal diet for human consumption, I use the precautionary principle and err on the side of caution. To apply the mindfulness in eating, use the precautionary principle and follow the practice of ahimsa. This practice is difficult for people to adopt with our fast paced society. To fully practice ahimsa, one must learn the art of stopping.

Americans are habituated to a materialistic lifestyle and are always on the go. There is a restless energy of constant doing and constant going. This constant running around is what makes people in modern industrialized societies feel alive. The fuel or food that keeps people running is material excess and overconsumption of things. This habit leads to the hedonic treadmill which causes unnecessary mental stress. There is never dedicated time for nourishing the soul. Multitasking has become the norm. Screen time has replaced real life three dimensional experiences. Eastern wisdom recommends the practice of stopping. Stop, unplug, and fully experience the here and the now. Once you stop, the next step is calming. This practice of stopping and calming allows for resting and healing. In the West, this only happens when one gets sick. If one is sick with influenza, then the natural cycle of stopping, resting and healing occurs. But should we wait to get sick to honor this cycle?

Nowadays, even the sacred act of eating is undermined by discussing the "things to do" in a business meeting, or going to a noisy restaurant and watching a band play, or any of the myriad distractions we have while eating. There is nothing inherently wrong with these activities; it is just that in America it has become the norm. This constant restlessness on external distractions instead of focusing on digestion can lead to the overconsumption of food. Ignoring the body's satiety center and signals to stop eating is a crime against the wisdom of millions of years of built in evolution. Our body orchestrates and synchronizes countless chemical reactions and releases hormones to help us assimilate our food. For example, the stomach and small intestine release ghrelin, the "hunger hormone," which helps regulate appetite. Once the stomach is stretched, the secretion of ghrelin stops. Obesity and overeating negatively impact this important hormone ghrelin that is associated with satiety, hedonic eating, metabolic and cardiovascular health, and is anti-aging. When we lose touch with these natural bodily signals, it leads to an overconsumption and disease. Distractions, or not eating mindfully, lead to not only overeating foods, but also to eating the wrong foods.

Hari Hachi Bu is a Confucian teaching that means "eat only until you are 80 percent full." Also, in Ayurveda, it is taught to eat the equivalent of your two hands opened in the shape of a bowl or offering. This amount is known as *anjali*, which also means "divine offering." Thus, we make the right offering to our divine selves. These ancient mindfulness principles can remind us we must honor natural body signals to keep a healthy body temple.

This practice is used regularly by the Okinawan elders and is thought to contribute to their exceptional longevity. Okinawans have the highest rate of centenarians per 100,000 people in the population, and this relative calorie restriction plays a role. They also have a very healthy body mass index (BMI). Mindful eating creates lightness and freedom to feel good by not overeating. Overeating is violence against our own body. Mindful eating is a practice of nonviolence and is self-compassion. Being mindful of consumption can be as simple as the ancient saying "eat when you are hungry and drink when you are thirsty." What may lead humans to overconsumption of food, and especially unhealthy foods, is determined by stress. Recent studies suggest that stress may compromise self-control. Stress in daily life and loss of self-control while eating has become the norm in our society.

Some Eastern traditions take eating mindfully to a whole new level. In the dining hall, there can be hundreds of monks eating their meals in complete silence. In this way, they are honoring the food. Eating in this fashion is meditation and a profound practice of ahimsa. The digestive fire, referred to as agni in Ayurveda, is fully focused on assimilating the nutrition entering the body. One mindful eating practice is to visualize the food in nature. If you are eating an apple, see the apple tree basking in the sun, the cool breeze shaking the leaves, and the rain nourishing its roots. With each bite, honor the interconnectedness of nature and all the elements and forces that allowed this wonderful fruit to sustain your body. You are what you eat and the atoms from the apple you eat will be incorporated into your body. When we eat mindfully, we see we are all interconnected. We respect and honor all life on earth, including our pets.

Let us take mindful eating to a whole new level by bringing this mindfulness to our beloved companion animals. In America, we view eating dog meat as taboo and we protect our dogs, for they are man's best friend. However, did you know even in America, it is legal in forty-four states to humanely kill one's dog and eat the dog meat for personal consumption? It is illegal to sell dog meat or serve it in restaurants in all fifty states. Does anyone reading this book view puppies as a delicacy? How about veal, which is calf meat? I would make a strong argument that eating dog meat or cow meat is equally harmful for the human body. Furthermore, if you find it acceptable to eat cow's meat but not acceptable to eat dog's meat, that is speciesist.

Speciesism is discrimination against animals. Discrimination is the highest form of arrogance. Anyone can be speciesist and discriminate against animals, irrespective of religious affiliation. For example, an atheist can say humans are at the top of the food chain and use "survival of the fittest" as the reason we could eat dog meat. A religious person might say, "God gave us dominion over all animals," as a reason to eat cow meat. At their core, all world religions teach peace, love, and being good stewards of the earth. If one considers cow meat and dog meat, we realize they are both the same. A heifer nurses and cares for her calf as a human mother feeds and nurtures her baby. A bitch nurses and protects her pups for as long as humans allow, too.

Mindful eating involves a shift in consciousness and embraces non-violence. It involves a realization we are all one big family. Modern science tells us all life on earth is interconnected. When we honor the planet, we only consume the blessings given to us and avoid over-consumption.

Controlling stress is also important to allow self-control in choosing the right foods. If we only consume what our body desires, from true hunger, we will naturally and effortlessly attain our ideal body weight. Research shows stress reduction and mindfulness can facilitate weight loss. If you eat mindfully and you are at your ideal weight, you will maintain it. If you are not at your ideal weight and eat mindfully, you will lose weight and attain your ideal weight spontaneously. The secret to a regular mindful eating practice is stress reduction. When we reduce stress, our cognition is clear and we honor the ancient practice of ahimsa.

Eating is a sacred act of connecting to the life force and energy of our universe through earth, wind, sun, and rain. Eat slowly in a mindful way and remember the ancient wisdom of Hari Hachi Bu (stop eating once your stomach is 80 percent full). Only eat an anjali, the portion size of your two hands cupped in the shape of a bowl. Eat only when you feel hunger signals from your body.

If you mindfully eat only what your body desires, you will naturally and effortlessly attain your ideal body weight. When we honor the planet, we only consume healthy plant food that the body needs and avoid over consumption. Controlling stress is crucial, so we can have the forethought to practice mindful eating every day. When practicing ahimsa, we carefully observe our thoughts, feelings and actions. We ensure that our thoughts, feelings, and actions are nonviolent. When we do so, we experience peace and promote health. Also, and as importantly, through living a life of ahimsa we promote health in our communities and the world.

As Mahatma Gandhi eloquently states:

> *Non-violence is not a garment to be put on and off at will. Its seat is in the heart, and it must be an inseparable part of our being.*

Live Your Truth

One Presence and
One Power

Validation Through
Meditation

Experience is Created
By Thoughts

Stardust in Everyone

CHAPTER 7

The Amazing Brain

> *That man is poor, not he who has little,*
> *but he who hankers after more.*
>
> —Seneca

THE HUMAN BRAIN IS AN AMAZING ORGAN. Neurobiologists estimate there are over 100 billion neurons in our brain with several hundred trillion synaptic connections. This is an enormous number of neuronal connections. The old paradigm in neuroscience stated that adults have a fixed number of neurons and cannot grow new brain cells. However, we now know adults, even well into old age, can create new neurons. This concept of the brain changing throughout the individual's life is known as neuroplasticity. Hebb's postulate summarizes how the brain changes through learning: *neurons that fire together, wire together.*

There are four broad categories of activities that promote brain health and even the creation of new brain cells: concentration and focused attention that is harnessed through meditation and mindfulness, aerobic exercise, novelty, and eating habits. These activities trigger brain-derived neurotrophic factor, a hormone that promotes neuronal growth.

The human brain has three major centers: the stress center, the pleasure center and the compassion center. One of the best strategies to keep a healthy brain is meditation and mindfulness. One of the worst things for our brains is chronic stress, which can lead to brain atrophy.

The stress center in your brain has been intricately designed to save your life under dangerous situations. However, left unchecked, chronic uncontrolled stress wreaks havoc on the body and leads to 80% of doctors visits. This stress response, also known as the fight, flight, freeze response, which releases adrenaline and cortisol is also known as the *rage reaction*. It originates in the amygdala. Unfortunately, in today's world we can experience this rage reaction with a 30 year mortgage, email inbox, traffic jams, or rude comment from a coworker. Historically, this stress system protected us from dangers in the jungle and not from petty, artificial constructs of our mind.

Chronic stress directly or indirectly leads to most modern diseases in industrialized societies. Meditation decreases stress hormones such as cortisol, epinephrine, and norepinephrine. The results are lower heart rate, lower blood pressure and decreased oxygen consumption. Through the practice of meditation one can decrease stress hormones, reduce anxiety, decrease inflammation, increase neuroplasticity, improve the immune system, and slow the aging process. Mindfulness allows one to live in the present moment thereby increasing happiness and joy. Meditation and mindfulness allows us to interpret and manage the stress of life in a healthy way and gives us the freedom to choose joy which engenders health. Neuroscientists have recently discovered that the default mode of the human brain is that of *mind wandering*. Some studies have found that our minds wander approximately 50 to 80% of the time. Mind wandering is associated with anxiety, depression and possibly dementia. One way to combat this restlessness of mind is through focused attention and concentration, meditation, and mindfulness.

The pleasure center in our brains reward us in a powerful way. In fact, we learned through the classic rat experiments in 1953, that the dopamine pleasure trap is so powerful, rats would ignore food and water in pursuit of pleasure. The rats in this experiment would press the lever to receive electrical stimulation of their brain and dopamine was released from the nucleus accumbens. The rats continued to press this lever for dopamine and ignored food and water to the point of death from exhaustion and starvation. This dopamine pleasure trap is a pathway for addictions. Addictions can be from anything that triggers the dopamine surge and includes gambling, eating, sex, drugs, internet, etc. However, this dopamine pleasure trap can manifest in other subtle ways. In our materialistic society many people associate happiness with acquisition of material objects. Indeed, the concept of the hedonic treadmill is when a person needs more and more consumption of material things to keep a low level of well being. This concept applies not only to our three dimensional lives and consumption of material objects. The hedonic treadmill can also apply to our digital lives. We need more and more electronic stimulation to feel the same level of happiness. One way to combat this pleasure trap is through the art of moderation. Also, temptations and toxic influences can be avoided through focused attention and concentration, meditation, and mindfulness.

The brain also has a compassion center. The hormone associated with the compassion center is the molecule of bliss or oxytocin released from the posterior pituitary gland. This is also known as the hug, bliss or love hormone. The major question that arises is toward whom should we express the most compassion? The most commonly overlooked concept is compassion should first start with oneself. Compassion toward yourself is key for a healthy mind and body and then one can express compassion to others. Once we express self-compassion and take care of our minds and bodies, then we heal.

When we nurture ourselves through self-care,

we engender peace and promote serenity. Serenity is the quality of living at ease, at peace and being fulfilled. Through self-compassion and self-care, we also engender contentment. Contentment is the quality of knowing true happiness comes from within. Contentment is when the mind, body and emotions are completely satisfied with the current moment. One is at ease. There is no external situation that could create true fulfillment. The practice of contentment is experiencing happiness, ease, and peace from within and not allowing any external circumstance to take this feeling away from you.

In Vedanta, this is also known as self-referral versus object-referral. If you are conditioned to seek happiness from material objects, then you are at the whim of the external world with all its ups and downs that come with chasing objects. You are on the hedonic treadmill. It is a roller coaster ride, a yo-yo effect, like the unpredictability of the stock market. It is not conducive to inner peace and contentment. However, with self-referral you are at peace, happy, and completely fulfilled since this state and feeling is generated from within. Here is a story that highlights the quality of self-referral or contentment.

Many years ago, there was a monk who lived in a small village. In this village, there was a 14-year-old girl who had become pregnant out of wedlock. Since no one in the village knew the young girl had a boyfriend, everyone accused the monk of being the sinner who got the girl pregnant. When the monk was accused, he merely stated, "Is that so?"

He continued on with his duties as monk and avoided all melodrama. He maintained an imperturbable mind in the midst of the external chaos. Then months later when the baby was born, the girl's family came to the monk and said, "Here, you take the baby and care for him and change his diapers and feed him. It will be your punishment."

The monk said, "Is that so?" He maintained an imperturbable mind. The monk cared for the baby with all his love and devotion. Two years passed.

Finally, the girl's boyfriend from a nearby village revealed himself and admitted that he was the father of the baby. The young girl's family came to the monk, apologetic and embarrassed, and said, "Give us the baby. We are sorry for what we put you through."

The monk said, "Is that so?"

The monk returned the baby to its parents with his blessings for their love and happiness.

The monk's peace and fulfillment came from his contentment within. It was not dependent on the vacillations of the outside world. He lived self-referral. This story does not illustrate complacency or cold detachment. In fact, it shows the opposite. Contentment leads to a fully engaged life. It is about accepting your current situation and doing your duty well without getting caught in melodrama or external distractions. Sometimes an external situation can be deceptive because most times there is more than meets the eye. Think back to a time in your own personal life when you had an apparent curse that turned out to be a blessing in disguise. We never know the plan the Universe has for us, she always surprises us in her mysterious ways.

An ancient Chinese story illustrates the illusions of outer appearances. There was a humble Chinese farmer who tilled his fields with an old horse. One day, the horse escaped into the countryside. The farmer's neighbors sympathized with him over his fate.

The farmer replied, "Bad luck? Good luck? Who knows?"

A week later the horse returned with a herd of wild stallions from the hills and this time the neighbors congratulated the farmer on his good luck.

The farmer replied, "Good luck? Bad luck? Who knows?"

When the farmer's son was attempting to tame one of the wild horses, he fell off and broke his leg. Everyone thought this was terrible luck.

The farmer's only reaction was "Bad luck? Good luck? Who knows?"

One week later, the Army marched into the village and required every healthy youth to enlist for war. When they saw the farmer's son with a broken leg, they let him stay at home.

Finally, the humble farmer said, "It could be good, it could be bad, all I can really say for certain is, I humbly accept what is happening now."

The story goes on and on with the ups and downs of a rollercoaster in life that is lived with object-referral. With object-referral, human beings are wallowing in despair or out of control with the agitation of euphoria and addiction.

Object-referral leads to the hedonic treadmill in which one needs more and more consumption of stuff for a low level of happiness. Through self-referral we discover a deep peace, equanimity and contentment with our current life situation and experience inner riches.

The Dali Lama says it well:

> *When you are discontent, you always want more, more, more. Your desire can never be satisfied. But when you practice content-ment, you can say to yourself, 'Oh yes – I already have everything that I really need.'*

CHAPTER 8

Meditation as Medication

Meditation is to be aware of every thought and of every feeling, never to say it is right or wrong, but just to watch it and move with it. In that watching, you begin to understand the whole movement of thought and feeling. And out of this awareness comes silence.
—Jiddu Krishnamurti

WHAT IF I TOLD YOU THAT THERE IS A MEDICATION that is all natural, free of side effects, that you can increase your dose at anytime, is available 24/7, and is free! Furthermore, this medication can delay aging, prevent and even reverse chronic disease, bring you peace and contentment! Would you take a daily dose? I am sure that your answer is "Yes." The great news is that there is a simple procedure that anyone can perform immediately. It is all natural, organic, free of side effects, and has a plethora of health benefits. Take a deep conscious breath in and then focus on consciously breathing out. Congratulations! That was your first dose!

Our nervous system has the opposite of the fight-or-flight response that is known as *rest and digest.* In this relaxed state, we have a decrease in stress hormones such as cortisol, epinephrine, norepinephrine, and increased nitric oxide. When our parasympathetic nervous system is stimulated, we have a lower heart rate, lower blood pressure and decreased oxygen consumption. The scientific procedure of meditation will produce a calm mind and a relaxed body and allow us to make excellent health choices.

We can measure the effects of meditation by looking at brain waves with an EEG machine. Beta waves are usually seen when eyes are open and alpha waves are usually seen with closed eyes in a more relaxed state. Theta and delta waves are found in deep sleep. The late Swami Satchidananda once had his brain waves measured to see how alpha waves can be captured. Since the Swami was a long time meditator, it was expected that the EEG machine would pick up predominantly alpha waves associated with relaxation. The researchers were embarrassed that the Swami did not have the expected waves. Then Swami Satchidananda calmly told the researchers perhaps they were looking for the wrong waves. The researchers were shocked to discover that while the swami was awake with his eyes open, he was in a state of deep relaxation with theta waves.

Astonishingly, these theta waves are seen in deep sleep but the Swami was awake! Such is the power of mindfulness and meditation.

The Harvard Professor Herbert Benson, M.D., coined the term *relaxation response* in the 1970s. It happens when we voluntarily activate our parasympathetic nervous system. The good news is that you do not have to be an advanced practitioner of meditation to reap the benefits. Dr. Benson has shown that even novice practitioners can reap immediate benefits from one session of relaxation response. Through one session of meditation, a practitioner can alter gene expression that decreases stress and inflammation. Dr. Benson's research showed that long-term meditators had 2,000 stress-reducing genes activated compared to those who do not meditate. The great news is that once novices learned to meditate for twenty minutes per day for eight weeks, they had activated 1,500 genes associated with stress reduction!

A study published in 2015 using biosensors to measure physiologic changes in both novice and experienced meditators found beneficial changes in brainwaves and blood pressure in both groups. It is not surprising that more and more studies are coming out showing a positive link between meditation and reduction in the aging process as measured by telomerase activity. These results show that chronic stress leads to premature aging at the cellular level. Also, chronic stress leads directly or indirectly to many chronic diseases that are associated with premature aging and an early death. There is exciting new research showing the effects of meditation on neuroplasticity and how meditation is exercise for the brain. How difficult is it to reap the benefits of meditation? Do you have to move to the Himalayan mountains and become a monk for a nine-month silent retreat and meditate in the lotus posture for eight hours a day to reap the benefits of neuroplasticity? The answer is "No."

Harvard neuroscientist Dr. Sara Lazar studied sixteen participants. After eight weeks, meditation strengthened many regions of the brain. The adage, "If you don't use it, you lose it" also applies to the brain, and this study shows that the meditators have healthier brains. The participants in this study were meditation naïve and used Mindfulness Based Stress Reduction (MBSR) as taught by Jon Kabat-Zinn, Ph.D. MBSR involves eight weekly group meetings and formal mindfulness training exercises. Mindfulness is defined as awareness of present moment experiences with a compassionate, nonjudgmental stance. Each day, the participants listened to a forty-five minute audio recording that guided them through body scan, yoga, and sitting meditation. The results suggest that MBSR can positively affect brain regions involved in learning, memory, emotional regulation, self-referential processing, and perspective taking.

The brain is a fascinating organ. Your brain has

100 billion neurons and 100 trillion connections. Although neuroplasticity is an exciting new field in neuroscience, the yogis have been talking about transforming the mind and body through the power of meditation for centuries. The late Paramahansa Yogananda discussed the power of meditation to transform the brain almost 100 years ago before functional MRI testing. In fact, the 2014 documentary *Awake: The Life of Yogananda* asserts that the yogi was discussing the process of neuroplasticity some 100 years before it was coined.

We know meditation can help strengthen the brain centers related to compassion. It naturally follows that Mahatma Gandhi was a yoga practitioner and practiced meditation daily. In fact, we can measure precisely the effects of different meditation techniques on different brain centers. Meditation is a form of all natural medication. Unfortunately, most Americans don't take advantage of this free and safe procedure. Instead, they support big pharma instead of relying on the free and natural pharmacology within our own bodies.

In America, one in five people take a psychiatric medication. We spend over 15 billion dollars on psychiatric drugs and billions more on mental health care. Meditation is a safe and effective modality that can help the mental health crisis. Recent studies show evidence for the use of meditation for psychological stress. Mindfulness meditation improves anxiety, depression, PTSD, pain, and mental health related quality of life. This is is exciting research! Meditation is a powerful tool you can perform at any time, anywhere, with no negative side effects. Another health crisis happening in America is the overdiagnosis and overtreatment of attention deficit disorder. There are studies in Europe showing that attention deficit disorder is more a product of social environment and parenting techniques than a pathology of the child's brain. For example, in the United States nine percent of school-age kids have a diagnosis of ADHD and take pharmaceuticals, whereas in France less than 0.5 percent have the diagnosis. The paradigm is different because the French look for an underlying cause in the social context but in America we view it as a pathological process. With mindfulness we can calm the restless chatter of the mind. Mindfulness can allow us to enhance our focus and attention naturally without pharmaceuticals.

What can we do to help a growing brain? A recent study explored how several meditation techniques affect the brain in terms of concentration. Researchers used concentration, Loving-Kindness, and Choiceless Awareness meditation practices to see how they impact mind-wandering, which is the default mode for humans. The premise is that mind-wandering correlates with unhappiness and that living in the present moment increases happiness. The researchers found that all three types of meditation techniques decreased mind-wandering both at baseline and during meditation. Imagine the benefits of teaching daily meditation practice in the school systems in America. If parents learned simple meditation techniques to help increase happiness and help decrease mind wandering, it is my professional opinion that there would be fewer diagnoses of attention deficit disorder. Also, parents can teach their children a simple breathing meditation technique that can be performed for one to two minutes every day that will help tremendously. One notable resource is MindUp™. This innovative, evidence-based program offered by The Hawn Foundation is teaching nearly 1 million children mindfulness techniques in schools all across the world.

Another concern in American healthcare is the overuse of narcotic painkillers. An estimated two million people abused prescription painkillers in 2013, according to the Center for Disease Control. Every year more people die from drug overdoses than from motor vehicle collisions. Chronic pain can be a problem but there are promising ways to help treat chronic pain that do not involve the toxic and potentially life-threatening side effects of taking a painkiller. Meditation also has implication to treat chronic pain. Recent studies have shown that meditators have increased brain size as shown via functional MRI. A study by Dr. Joshua Grant and colleagues published in 2010 studied seventeen meditators with eighteen controls. Meditators had significantly lower pain sensitivity which was associated with having a thicker cortex in the anterior cingulate and in the somatosensory cortex. Instead of going directly to a dangerous and potentially deadly narcotic drugs to treat pain, physicians should consider the safer modality of meditation.

Reducing stress is one of the most important things an individual can do for overall health and especially heart health. Every day in the United States 2,200 people die of cardiovascular disease. Health care expenditures are $316.6 billion annually to treat heart disease and stroke. It has been known for decades there are higher incidences of heart attacks and strokes on Monday more than any other day of the week. Why? It is postulated that the stress hormones released in preparing for the work week increase blood pressure, arrhythmias, and inflammation.

What can be done about this? Meditate every day and especially on weekends when one has more free time to prepare for the week. Meditation is beneficial to the body by strengthening the brain regions to help combat stress, decrease C-reactive protein, improve perception and neural response to pain, improve immune function, and lower blood pressure. There are countless studies showing that meditation can positively affect neuroplasticity.

Meditation can give you a stronger and more resilient brain better able to handle stress. Stress will always be the universal presence in human life. The question is how one will interpret it and process it.

By practicing meditation, we can deal with life stress in a more effective way. There will always be a dance between pain and joy in life. Meditation allows us to handle both artistically. In Dr. Joseph Campbell's work, he notes that life has equal parts pain and pleasure, tragedy and comedy. The great philosophers from ancient times observed a continuum of pleasure and pain. Similarly, Dr. Campbell has observed in mythologies throughout history a continuum of tragedy and comedy. In Vedic thought, it is Maya, the cosmic play, the magic show of the universe. This insight will allow us to handle life challenges in a more effective way.

The experience of childbirth illustrates this point. Childbirth is a very painful experience. However, from this pain an enormous joy is produced from the birth of a baby. Similarly, a delicious food can produce great joy. Conversely, eating too much of this food can produce pain and suffering. In the long term, overindulgence can lead to addiction. Indeed, Dr. Campbell states, "We cannot cure the world of sorrow, but we can choose to live in joy."

Meditation and mindfulness allow us to interpret and manage the pain and stress of life in a healthy way and give us the freedom to choose joy. The first aspect of meditation is to stop. Stop the running here and there, day and night. After stopping, the practitioner calms the mind through mindful breathing meditation, allowing the mind and body to rest and heal. This whole process can take just a few minutes. The direct result of this practice is that stress hormones are reduced and the rate of aging slows. The indirect result is that when confronted with a stimulus that, in the past, would have led to sadness and overeating, the practitioner now becomes aware and witnesses the emotions without mindlessly reacting. It is important to note that emotional turbulence can involve the restlessness that comes from excitement, happiness, agitation, and sadness, etc., which can take away mental peace and emotional equanimity.

If we find we have lost our inner peace and lost our equanimity, then we should not proceed with whatever activity we are engaged in until we have found our center. For example, if you have become angry or lonely or sad it would not be an ideal time to eat your meal. Wisdom would be to observe the inner turbulence and skip a meal or wait until you have found your calm center. Here is a brief memory tool that can be used as a self-knowledge or mindfulness tool. For more details on mindfulness and meditation techniques refer to my book, *Three Steps to Superior Health: An Evidence-Based Guide for Stress Reduction, Longevity, and Weight Loss.*

A mnemonic device to help you remember the principle of witnessing any emotional turbulence when it surfaces is to think of: **HALT REAL Insight**. Each letter stands for a word to help you remember to observe your emotions and thoughts before reacting and will give you the freedom to choose.

Hunger: Is hunger the source of your irritability and temper?

Anger: Are you angry and is this causing you to project your issues onto another person?

Lonely: Is loneliness causing you to overeat and create food addictions?

Tired: Are you tired, and this is leading to crankiness and poor health decisions?

Recognize: After you have observed your emotions with HALT, if you are sad, just recognizing that you are sad is the first step to healing.

Embrace: Once you recognize that you are sad, angry, lonely, etc., embrace this emotion and own up to this feeling.

Accept: Once you have recognized it and embraced it, you are no longer in denial, and you can accept it for what it is, a feeling or thought.

Look deeply: Once you have recognized it, embraced it, and accepted this emotion or thought, you can look deeply into its root cause.

Insight: Once you have gone through the procedure of HALT REAL, you will spontaneously have insight into yourself and feel better right away.

Imagine you are a traveler on the train carrying a heavy backpack. You remain standing with a heavy backpack. The train picks up speed, and it's going seventy-five mph, and it will arrive at its destination in twenty-four hours. But as the train is traveling, you are still standing and holding on to your heavy backpack. A wise man who is sitting in the train looks at you and says, "Why don't you let go of that heavy backpack and sit down? Have a seat and enjoy the journey!" The backpack is a metaphor for human suffering.

Life is always filled with heavy backpacks. The key is to learn to put down the heavy burden of the backpack. Let the train carry your heavy load and guide you to your next destination. Let go of stress and enjoy the journey. We do so by using meditation as our all-natural medication. When we harness this free inner resource we directly combat chronic stress. Chronic stress directly or indirectly leads to most modern diseases in industrialized societies. Meditation decreases stress hormones such as cortisol, epinephrine, and norepinephrine. This leads to lower heart rate, lower blood pressure, and decreased oxygen consumption. Through the practice of meditation one can decrease stress hormones, reduce anxiety, decrease inflammation, increase neuroplasticity, improve the immune system, and slow the aging process. Mindfulness allows one to live in the present moment thereby increasing happiness. Meditation and mindfulness allow us to interpret and manage the stress of life in a healthy way and give us the freedom to choose joy and engender health.

CHAPTER 9

Mindfulness Breaks the Vicious Cycle

If you change the way you look at things,
the things you look at change.

—Wayne Dyer

I AWAKE AT MY USUAL ZERO DARK THIRTY. THE routine is simple: brush teeth, make coffee, and use the restroom. Then I do my formal meditation practice, kiss the wife, and prepare to start the day. There is a strange and eerie feeling about this morning. As I sip on hot coffee, my eye catches the NY Times headline news that is startling: Humans Have 24 Hours Left To Live: Life On Earth Will Be Annihilated By A Massive Asteroid! Utterly shocked, I reread the headline five times as my hands tremble. I thought it must be a typo, or a bad joke. It was not. Scientists identified a massive asteroid, the size of Africa, traveling at Mach 131, an astounding 100,000 MPH! This massive asteroid would hit the earth in twenty-four hours and life as we know it, in the goldilocks of our universe, would vanish! The top scientists and military powers from around the world, are utterly hopeless, and have no answer to this impending catastrophic event.

My mind is restless and running everywhere. Moe is calmly staring intently at my facial expression. I immediately feel more relaxed by his deep gaze through the mystery of mirror neurons. Moe is a three-year-old silent working dog: a fifty-five pound, handsome blue heeler. His ears are at attention, and he is in the sphinx pose, all four paws flat on the floor, and focused only on me. Nothing in his world matters more than looking at my face. Over tens of thousands of years, dogs have evolved an exquisite ability to read their owner's face. He is calm, relaxed, silent and fully present. Then he immediately expresses empathy, and tilts his head to the side, as he reads my concerned facial expression. He is utterly oblivious to the massive asteroid and our impending doom. His only concern is my face at this moment.

I ask myself, would Moe change anything in his last twenty-four hours of life? The answer was a resounding "No!" He would live this last twenty-four hours like his previous ones. He would offer unconditional love and be fully immersed in the present moment. He would offer unconditional devotion and make me feel like the most special person on earth. He would guard, protect, and love me today, our last day, just as he has done every single day for the past two years. Today is no different.

Then I woke up from my dream… And there was Moe, watching me silently and lovingly, as I lifted my head from the pillow.

Ironically, this dream was not a terrifying nightmare. This dream offered tremendous insight: a gift from man's best friend. Dogs live every day to the fullest without regret. They offer unconditional love, companionship, and loyalty from dawn till dusk. With each wet kiss they are saying, "I love you." If you step out of the house for two minutes, they are overjoyed when they see you again. The next day they get up and repeat the same.

Humans could learn a great lesson from our companion animals. They live in the here and now. They do not stress out about the past or the future. Because of this present moment awareness, they have an inner calm and peace that is healing.

Dogs offer us a portal for healing by tapping into our relaxation response for stress reduction. They are a perfect living example of peace, calm and relaxation. Humans try to imitate this calm and relaxed nature that dogs exude. Across America, countless humans can be found doing the downward and upward dog, which are yoga postures to help engender relaxation. Our companion animals know how to experience peace and calm effortlessly. They live fully every day. They are the living embodiment of the famous quote, "Live everyday as if it were your last, because one of these days, it will be." I would extend this to not just each day, but down to each minute and second of every day. Though the power of present moment awareness we stop living like robots.

Meditation and mindfulness increase one's willpower and freedom to choose. Most people live their lives in a very reactionary way. They walk around life aimlessly, like lifeless robots, letting external life circumstances determine their destiny. There is a stimulus (someone harshly criticizes you) and an immediate response (you angrily get defensive). Many times, this response comes without forethought. Of course, there are stimulus-response scenarios that are normal and physiologic, like the stimulus of a hot stove and the response of immediately moving the hand. What about the stimulus of a negative thought, past hurt, and emotional pain? Do these thoughts and feelings immediately trigger the response of smoking, drinking, or overeating to numb the pain? For many people, this scenario is exactly what happens and they are not even aware of it!

There is no space between stimulus and response. Meditation and mindfulness create space and enlarge the conscious awareness between stimulus and response. With this space and heightened consciousness comes the freedom to choose your next action (response), and ideally you choose the miracle (positive). The next time that a negative thought, past hurt, or emotional pain comes, the secret is to become aware of it, and realize that those thoughts and feelings are not the real you. Then, transform those old grievances by choosing something positive in the miracle of the present moment. You can do something positive like exercising or reading, or just be with yourself and focus on the breath until the thoughts and feelings go away. This process is also known as the eternal witness. The late Stephen R. Covey said it well, "Between stimulus and response is our greatest power—the freedom to choose."

There is a powerful quote by Dr. Viktor Frankl in his classic book *Man's Search For Meaning*, "Everything can be taken from a man but one thing: the last of the human freedoms—to choose one's attitude in any given set of circumstances, to choose one's own way." It is astonishing that Dr. Frankl remained positive, even in the horrors of a Nazi concentration camp. His choice of attitude allowed him to survive. The secret of mindfulness is to observe your thoughts and emotions as they surface and become aware of them in a nonjudgmental way. After a short while, you release them. They are not there to stay. You let them go, and they go away. A mnemonic device to help you remember the principle of witnessing any emotional turbulence when it surfaces is to think of HALT REAL Insight. With mindfulness, we are accessing the power of now.

Rumi, the great Sufi poet, eloquently describes mindfulness and the power of acceptance:

> *This being human is a guest house*
> *Every morning a new arrival.*
> *A joy, a depression, a meanness,*
> *some momentary awareness comes*
> *as an unexpected visitor.*
> *Welcome and entertain them all!*
> *Even if they are a crowd of sorrows,*
> *who violently sweep your house*
> *empty of its furniture,*
> *still treat each guest honorably.*
> *He may be clearing you out for some new delight.*
> *The dark thought, the shame, the malice,*
> *meet them at the door laughing,*
> *and invite them in.*
> *Be grateful for whoever comes,*
> *because each has been sent*
> *as a guide from beyond.*

Live Your Truth

One Presence and One Power

Validation Through Meditation

Experience is Created By Thoughts

Stardust in Everyone

CHAPTER 10

Thoughts Have The Power To Shape Your Reality

The one and only formative power given to man is thought.
By his thinking he not only makes character, but body and
affairs, for as he thinketh within himself, so is he.

—Charles Fillmore

ONCE UPON A TIME, AN ENLIGHTENED FARMER WAS working in the field. He lived in a very peaceful serene village and he wanted to keep it that way. He reflected on his life and realized that he had shaped his reality through his attitude and positive thinking. At that moment, a traveler from a nearby village came walking down the long dirt path. The traveler had intentions to move to the farmer's village.

Once he got close enough he asked the farmer, "How are the people in this village?"

The farmer replied, "How were the people from where you lived before?"

The traveler said, "Oh, they were generous, grateful, kind, loving people. I will miss them dearly."

The farmer said, "That is exactly how the people

are here. You are welcome here anytime."

Shortly thereafter, another traveler came down the dirt path who was from the same village as the previous traveler, and asked the farmer, "How are the people in this village?"

The farmer replied, "How were the people from where you lived before?"

The second traveler said, "Oh, they were mean, rude, disrespectful, stingy, and so ungrateful. I am happy to leave them."

The farmer said, "That is exactly how the people are in this village. You will not like it here."

The two travelers were given different answers to the same question. Their individual subjective experiences colored their opinions. This story illustrates the power of our minds to create reality. Indeed, we can transform our lives if we cultivate positive thoughts and feelings of gratitude. Even the simple things in life can generate joy and happiness.

Obtain a blank sheet of paper. Write all the things for which you are grateful. If starting this exercise is difficult for you, imagine you have fully recovered from being a quadriplegic for the past year. If you could fully use your body again for the first time in a long time, what would you be thankful for? For example, you can start with your body. I am grateful for my eyes that allow me to see a burst of colors and myriad shapes. I am grateful for my hearing that allows me to hear the sound of children playing and birds chirping. I am grateful for my nose that allows me to smell spring flowers and home cooking. I am grateful for my legs that allow me to walk. I am grateful for my tongue that allows me to taste delicious food and say sweet words.

With this simple gratitude practice you can fill many pages by just scanning your body from head to toe and stating all the things you are thankful for. Also, write friends, family, co-workers, neighbors, church members, etc. for which you are grateful. This exercise can be as simple as writing three things every morning for which you are grateful. Giving thanks and being grateful for things in your life then becomes a habit. Studies have shown that gratitude practice can improve health, happiness, and relationships.

Einstein said it well, "There are only two ways to live your life. One is as though nothing is a miracle. The other is as though everything is a miracle."

All events and situations can be viewed as a choice between a grievance or a miracle. The art is to choose the miracle. The present moment has many conditions of joy and happiness available to feel grateful for being alive. This present moment is a miracle.

Modern psychology has proven that happiness that comes from within is profound and enduring. Happiness that comes from outside ourselves is fleeting. A classic example is the study in 1978 from Northwestern University and University of Massachusetts on the happiness of lottery winners versus paraplegics one year later. We know both lottery winners and paraplegics have the same baseline level of happiness one year later. After winning the lottery, the novelty rapidly wore off. The new things that the winners accumulated brought a transient happiness. After a short period, the thrill of extra money wore off, and they became accustomed to their new life. This effect is known as hedonic adaptation. In fact, the researchers discovered that the paraplegics had more pleasure from everyday activities such as talking with friends, watching TV, eating, and laughing at a joke.

There is another classic study that shows the power of positive psychology. For The Nun Study, psychologists analyzed the biographical essays of 180 Nuns from when they first entered the convent at the average age of 22. They also analyzed journal entries from throughout the nuns' lives and found that the nuns that were more optimistic and happier lived up to 10 years longer. The cheerful sisters had a significantly higher likelihood to live into their 80s and 90s than the less cheerful sisters.

We know from the memoirs of Louis Zamperini and Dr. Victor Frankl that positive thinking enhances your chances of survival under extreme stress as a prisoner of war. Manufacturing happiness from within also brings health, longevity, and pleasure from mundane everyday activities. Modern day research is giving us evidence through long term studies what ancient sages have known for millennia. Any situation, no matter how extreme, can be transformed with the power of thinking.

Consider two inmates condemned to a life sentence. They both are confined to the same small room, and each has a tiny window to peer out to the world. Each day, they both grab the bars and peek outside their jail cell. One looks down at the dirt, mud, worms and cesspool on the ground and feels miserable, depressed, morose, dejected and suicidal. The other, looking up at the expansive blue sky and brilliant sun feels freedom, joy, exhilaration and infinite bliss. The two prisoners have the same external situations yet they have different inner experiences.

The concept of true joy and happiness coming from within ourselves versus the illusion of happiness coming from name, fame, and money was eloquently described 2,500 years ago. Lao Tzu in the *Tao Te Ching* Verses 44 states:

> *Fame or integrity: which is more important?*
> *Wealth or happiness: which is more valuable?*
> *Success or failure: which is more destructive?*
>
> *If you look to others for fulfilment,*
> *you will never truly be fulfilled.*
> *If your happiness depends on accumulating wealth,*
> *you will never truly be happy.*

What you gain is more trouble
than what you lose.
Be content with what you have;
rejoice in the way things are.
If you know when to stop
and realise there is nothing lacking,
the whole world belongs to you.

It is through the power of positive thinking one can transform reality. Positive affirmations are a proven way to rewire your brain and release healing hormones in your body. When we state a positive affirmation silently or out loud we create a special energy that helps break destructive stagnant patterns. Words have immense power to initiate a healing cycle. One must become conscious of the intimate cycle of thoughts, words, and deeds. Here are examples of positive affirmations from Unity Worldwide:

"I hold the keys to my own prosperity."

"My mind and body are whole, well, and strong."

If you repeat these positive affirmations regularly, they have a powerful effect on your mind and body.

We have discussed strategies to control our thoughts through the eternal witness technique, mindfulness, and meditation. Also, one can practice gratitude daily to generate health and develop better interpersonal relationships. Next, let us explore the power of words to create your destiny.

Every spiritual tradition places the utmost importance on right speech. Words have the power of magic. Words spoken at the right time, in the right way, can create something wonderful. Think back to a time when a friend was having a bad day, and you gave them a compliment and brightened up their day. In an instant, just a few simple words changed a friends feelings from sadness to joy. Sweet speech is like alchemy, transforming base feelings to gold. On the other hand, negative speech has the power to hurt and create lifelong emotional scars. Many times hurtful speech hurts more than any physical pain. One strategy is to heed Gandhi's famous words, "Speak only if it improves upon silence." Another approach is to follow the Toltec wisdom as described by Don Miguel Ruiz: if you must speak, be impeccable with your word. Once you utter a hurtful word that is not impeccable, you cannot take it back. An old proverb explains this point.

Once upon a time, a man was cruel with his word and went around spreading lies and saying mean things about other people. He had mastered the art of gossip. Then he realized that many people were distancing themselves from him. His business and relationships were suffering. He consulted a wise sage and asked for help on how he could undo all the hurtful words he said. The sage asked the man to grab a bag of feathers, go to the edge of a deep oceanside cliff and empty the bag of feathers. The sage then asked the man to return the next day to see him. The next day the sage said, "Now go gather all the feathers."

The man said, "It is impossible. The wind has spread the feathers far and wide. I cannot bring them back."

The wise sage nodded, "Your words are like the feathers. Once you release them it is impossible to bring them back."

Controlling your speech is only half the battle. Our peace and equanimity can be affected by other people's hurtful words. There is a simple yet profound strategy on dealing with someone's anger and hurtful words that are directed at you: Do not accept another person's anger. Once you do, you have accepted it as a gift. In fact, when you accept another person's anger and take things personally your ego is impeding your happiness.

The Buddha was walking in a village. A mean and rude man came up to him and hurled insults at the Buddha. The mean man said, "You are fake and a fraud. You are not qualified to teach!" He continued, "In fact, you are too young to have any wisdom and you are a bastard child!"

The Buddha remained calm and kept his equanimity. The Buddha asked the mean man, "Tell me, if you buy a gift for someone, and that person does not take it, to whom does the gift belong?"

The man was perplexed by such a strange question and could not believe how calm the Buddha remained. He said, "It would belong to me, because I bought the gift."

The Buddha wore a serene smile and said, "Now, you have just cursed me. But if I do not accept your curses, if I do not get insulted and angry in return, these curses will fall back upon you—the same as the gift returning to its owner."

When other people try to put us down and insult us let's remember this simple strategy. Don't accept it. The moment we take an insult personally and get defensive is the moment we let our egos impede our happiness. The key is to generate happiness from within. We do so by avoiding the dangerous pattern of associating our happiness with external objects. If our happiness depends on external objects, we are on the hedonic treadmill. This habit creates dissatisfaction, pain, and suffering in life also known as dukkha in Buddhism. Once we have become conscious of our thoughts and words, then we must focus on our deeds.

Love is a verb. It is an action. Regardless of what our minds and emotions are telling us, we can shape our reality through our actions. A well known strategy in behavioral psychology is "fake it 'til you make it." If you want to create your reality, live your life and take actions as if you already have what you desire. One way to directly change your life is with the power of habit through action. When we positively influence our thoughts, words, and deeds, we become the masters of our destiny. To transform our lives takes work. Most people don't just roll out of bed and walk through the challenges of life seeing everything as glass half full. This takes practice through meditation and mindfulness. Also one must nourish and generate happiness from within. These universal principles require active participation for them to come alive in your life. The daily practice is part of the journey and should be fun.

Thich Nhat Hanh shares this inspirational wisdom:

> *Because suffering is impermanent, that is why we can transform it. Because happiness is impermanent, that is why we have to nourish it.*

Live Your Truth

One Presence and
One Power

Validation Through
Meditation

Experience is Created
By Thoughts

Stardust in Everyone

CHAPTER 11

The Power Of Social Networks

Through Love all that is bitter will be sweet,
Through Love all that is copper will be gold,
Through Love all dregs will become wine,
Through Love all pain will turn to medicine.

—Rumi

THE PARALLELS OF OUR HUMAN BODY AND THE universe are amazing. Our brain has 100 billion neurons and our Milky Way has 100 billion stars. 71% of Earth's surface is water and about 70% of the human body is water. The electron cloud of atoms in our body mimics the motion of the planets. Scientists have discovered that of the trillions of atoms in our body, up to 93%, come from stardust. In fact, 98% of the atoms in your body are replaced every year and exchanged with atoms from our universe. The atoms that one year ago were in a person living in Africa, China, Mexico, etc. may now be atoms in your body today. All of humanity is connected in such a profound way. The writers of the Upanishads had a similar insight into the nature of reality thousands of years earlier:

As is the human body, so is the cosmic body.
As is the human mind, so is the cosmic mind.
As is the microcosm, so is the macrocosm.
As is the atom, so is the universe.

Our biorhythms are connected to the rhythms of nature. This natural biorhythm should be honored. There is a time to sleep, to wake, to eat, to rest, etc. When we honor this natural rhythm in life, we maintain harmony and ease in our body. When we don't honor it, we create dis-ease in our body.

When you recognize that we all are made from the same stuff, namely stardust, you recognize that we are all connected at a deeper level. From this cosmic perspective, the word *Namaste*, "the light within me honors the light within you," takes on a special meaning. This knowledge allows you to connect with others, forming a social network of like-minded people. We form our *Sangha*, good association, and this promotes health and longevity. We have 100 years of data showing that a social network promotes longevity.

Intriguingly, there is evidence that your friends influence your body weight. The closer your relationship, the more impact it will have on your body weight. According to multiple studies, the adage, "Birds of a feather flock together" remains true for weight. I had a patient who is morbidly obese, and he confessed that all of his friends are also obese. Since he is the "biggest" out of all of his friends, he is given the most food. A lot of the affection and "love" that he received from his obese friends was in the form of food, and he had a difficult time refusing this affection. If you will make a stand for your health, you need the courage to say "no" to your current friends that engage in harmful behavior. If your friends don't support you in your new health plan, then you need to find friends who will. Too much food, just like too much alcohol will eventually kill you and should be considered a poison of sorts. An alcoholic who would like to get sober should not be immersed with alcoholic friends and going to bars. If you want to improve your health and change your reality, socialize with friends who have the same goals and are of like mind. Anyone can change their life for the better.

There is a legend of Ratnakar, a highway robber and murderer. He claimed he was committing these awful sins to support his family. He was under the false assumption that his family would share responsibility for his sins since he was doing it for them. Narada, a great sage, advised him to ask his family whether they agreed to share the burden. When Ratnaker asked them, he was shocked to discover no one in his family supported him in his crimes. He was all alone in absorbing his sins and the karmic consequences. Upon this realization, he stopped living his life as a criminal and studied the universal teachings of inner freedom and liberation.

Sage Narada then gave him a sacred mantra to help him attain enlightenment. He was given the mantra of Rama. Ratnakar, who had lived his entire life as a criminal, could not repeat "Rama," a holy name of God. He felt he was unworthy of repeating such a pure and divine name since he had committed so many acts of evil in his lifetime. Sage Narada, in his wisdom, instructed him to use "Mara" instead. Mara, which is a demon and symbolizes death, was easy for Ratnaker to chant. After many years of diligent spiritual practice and chanting "MaraMaraMara" the sound ran together and became "RamaRama Rama!" Ratnakar was then spiritually enlightened and became Sage Valmiki. Sage Valmiki wrote the Ramayana and Yoga Vashista and was a dedicated servant of God. It came to be because Ratnaker found *satsang* with Sage Narada. Sage Narada saw the potential of the criminal Ratnaker. Although Ratnaker had within him the potential to be a star, he was living a life of crime that obscured his star from shining. Once that starlight within is nurtured, we fulfill our highest potential by shining bright and serving humanity. All humans have an amazing light within that should be harnessed so we can fulfill our highest potential. One of the best ways to accomplish this is through satsang.

The Sanskrit word *satsang* is derived from "true" and "company." Satsang is good association and being in the company of the highest truth. There is nothing more important than being united and in harmony with a group of people who are in search of the highest truth. Everyone deserves their natural inheritance of living their truth and being healthy and happy. Unity Church recognizes there is a spark of divinity in everyone. When we keep good association of like-minded followers, it will lead to health, happiness, and longevity. In fact, good association is so powerful, that Sage Vashistha calls it a portal to liberation. In Buddhism, the Sangha is one of the three jewels of the practice. Proverbs 13:20 makes it clear: *He who walks with wise men will be wise, but the companion of fools will suffer harm.*

Once we have found our social network, we must continue accepting, loving and being kind to other people. There is no extremism or exclusivity. Strangers who want to join your practice should be welcomed. To form a deep connection to others, silently repeat "Namaste" to yourself every time your eyes meet with a stranger's. With this practice, you are saying, "The starlight within me honors the starlight within you." You realize that you and the stranger come from the same stuff, stardust. As Jesus said, "Love your neighbor as yourself." It is tangible since we are all intimately interconnected. The thread that connects us all is love.

CHAPTER 12

Self-Compassion

If you don't love yourself, you cannot love others. You will not be able to love others. If you have no compassion for yourself then you are not able of developing compassion for others.

—Dalai Lama

COMPASSION TOWARD YOURSELF IS THE MOST important thing one can do for a healthy mind and body. We cannot express compassion toward others adequately without first having self-compassion or self-love. Once we express self-compassion and take care of our minds and bodies, then we are fulfilled and healthy. Only then do we have the energy and capacity to serve others. To do this, we must escape from the bad habits that create chronic stress and addiction. When we constantly try to please other people without self-regard, we enter the pressure cooker of chronic stress. Then, to control the chronic stress that is self-created one self-soothes with bad habits. Bad habits come in many forms, such as eating junk food, not exercising, always saying yes to others, too much alcohol, drugs, taking tranquilizers for stress and sleep, and internet addiction.

How do we escape from the bad habits, addictions, and chronic stress? We do so through self-compassion. When we nurture ourselves through self-care, we engender peace and promote a healthy mind and body. Self-care is not a sign of weakness but a sign of strength. When we have self-care, we form a strong foundation in our body temple. We must take care of our physical bodies first if we want to be healthy and achieve the highest goal.

The Buddha said, "Your body is precious. It is our vehicle for awakening. Treat it with care."

Self-care is a powerful way of honoring your body. What does self-care look like? I will list activities that should be done every day that form the foundation of self care. This list is not exhaustive and may change depending on your life circumstances or physical or mental disabilities. A healthy daily self-care plan involves:

Eight hours of sleep.

Thirty to sixty minutes of exercise.

Fifteen minutes of meditation.

Eating a healthy whole-foods plant-based diet.

Not smoking or doing drugs.

Not drinking alcohol in excess.

Practicing mindfulness throughout the day.

Through self-compassion we engender wellness and contentment. When we have contentment, there is no external situation that could take that feeling away. The practice of contentment is experiencing happiness, ease, and peace from within. Do not allow any external circumstance to take this feeling away from you. By practicing self-compassion we develop the capacity to feel the joy and happiness that originates from within. Once we experience happiness from within, we are immune to criticism, blame, flattery, and shame. This is the power of self-compassion.

Seeking happiness from outside of yourself leads to pain and suffering. Pain because the body gets damaged by years of neglect and abuse. Suffering because the mind is constantly chasing after more material objects and is on the hedonic treadmill. As Seneca once eloquently pointed out, "That man is poor, not he who has little, but he who hankers after more." This is materialism.

With materialism you are conditioned to seek happiness from material objects. But also, you seek happiness from less tangible things such as other people's opinion, the internet, net worth, power, social rank, title, and diplomas. You are at the whim of the external world with all its ups and downs that come with chasing objects and things outside of you. It is a roller coaster ride, a yo-yo effect, like the unpredictability of the stock market. You can never experience lasting joy and equanimity of mind. It is not conducive to inner peace and contentment.

However, with the practice of self-compassion you are at peace, happy and completely fulfilled since this state and feeling is self-generated. A plethora of peer-reviewed research studies shows that self-compassion fosters wellbeing. I have created a mnemonic device whose acronym is self-compassion, each letter stands for something powerful that you can do every day to remind you that self-care is instrumental: S.E.L.F.-C.O.M.P.A.S.S.I.O.N.

S: Self-care seven days per week

Self-care should not be reserved only for vacations, weekend getaways, when you retire, when the kids grow up, when you make more money, when you have more time, etc. It should start today and be a daily practice. In fact, all the self-care practices discussed are free and will save you money. More important than financial savings, it will bring inner riches and wellbeing.

E: Energy conservation

Self-care is about balance and moderation. When training for a marathon one doesn't run 26.2 miles every day during training. There are much shorter runs and there are days off for rest. The goal is to peak on race day. Similarly, life is like a long marathon. Our training should be steady and regular for success. If success in the end is a long life filled with rich experiences and joy, then we must conserve our energy. Many spend all of their energy on others and self-sabotage their own health. Others are narcissistic, using all their energy on omphaloskepsis and are narcissistic. There is a sweet spot in energy conservation. If we set aside some energy every day for self-renewal we become better vessels for helping others and completing the metaphorical marathon of life.

L: Love yourself

Love is a verb. To love yourself, you have to be proactive and take action! Schedule a daily exercise routine, regular massage therapy, tea/coffee dates with friends, and regular time off where you do nothing. Taking a day off and doing nothing is gentle loving gesture for yourself. Whereas working every day without time for rest will lead to chronic stress, disease and a premature death.

F: Forgive yourself and others

As humans we all make mistakes. Even computers make mistakes. The difference is that when humans make mistakes, we continually punish ourselves countless times over a previous error. When you forgive yourself and others for mistakes, you discover freedom. Holding onto a grudge, anger, and lack of forgiveness is bondage. A prison you carry with you wherever you go. Remember the saying, "When you forgive you set the prisoner free, then you realize the prisoner was you!"

C: Cannot please everyone

One of the most harmful behavioral patterns is the constantly saying yes to every request and sacrificing our own health. People who constantly say yes to friends, family, coworkers, supervisors, church members, volunteerism, etc., end up overextending themselves and suffering from burnout. There is no conservation of energy for self-care. One's personal health is sabotaged, and this leads to a plethora of acute and chronic diseases.

O: Observe your thoughts

Observing your thoughts moment to moment in a nonjudgmental way is mindfulness. When we can observe our thoughts without reacting to them we discover that we are the masters of our destiny. If we are not mindful of our thoughts, we become a slave to the restless mind, emotions, and desires. Mindfully observing our thoughts creates space for self-care. If we react to our every thought, we create disease. As Shakespeare succinctly says it, "Give thy thoughts no tongue." Many of today's politicians should heed this advice.

M: Meditate daily

A daily practice of formal meditation of about 15 minutes engenders health and is one of the highest forms of self-care. This practice allows for a spaciousness to choose your response in any situation. Meditation increases your willpower to be a conscious choice maker in orchestrating the life of your dreams. Many people are stuck in a vicious pattern of stimulus followed by an immediate reaction. This cycle engenders endless pain. Meditation transforms this cycle. The cycle becomes stimulus, followed by a space to choose the highest response. By mindfully choosing the highest response you enter a cycle in which you are a conscious choice maker. As a conscious choice maker you create the life of your dreams.

P: Practice every day and avoid perfectionism

The key to success in any meaningful endeavor is daily practice. Avoid perfectionism which creates unnecessary pressure and stress. Even great musicians and athletes practice regularly knowing there is always room for improvement. Remember the aphorism, "the perfect is the enemy of the good." Try your best in self-care every day and that is good enough. Do not expect a perfect day of meditation, eating, exercising, weather, etc. Go with the flow of things in life and be flexible. This way, you will be more focused on the practice, the effort, the journey and not some shangrila perfect destination. Practice every day at trying your best and being good and you will succeed. Remember Cubs manager Joe Maddon's famous double entendre, "Don't ever permit the pressure to exceed the pleasure."

A: Associate with like-minded people

When we associate with like-minded people, we harness a special energy that allows for health and healing. Many cultures and religions have satsang or good association as a form of transforming our lives for a higher good. In this atmosphere, there is an energy that facilitates breaking bad habits and addictive behaviors. If we hang around drug addicts and chain smokers every day, then we will likely succumb to these addictions. If you want to live a clean life free of addictions choose your friends wisely. Think of the Japanese proverb, "When the character of a man is not clear, look at his friends."

S: Self-criticism should be avoided

Stop harshly criticizing yourself. On this long journey of life, you will make mistakes. Accept your mistakes and learn from them. Most importantly, be kind and gentle with yourself and forgive. Research shows that harsh self-criticism leads to isolation which leads so self-absorption. Don't isolate yourself from others until sometime in the future when you are perfect. Go out into the world and open yourself up to new experiences that allow you to grow. Don't expect that self-absorption in five hours of daily meditation will make you a better person. Don't be self-absorbed and think because you're a raw food vegan you're better than everyone who is not. Self criticism, isolation, and self-absorption are pathways to sabotaging your health.

S: Sleep eight hours per day

You are a warrior. In daily life you have battles and challenges in the form of paying bills, work, disgruntled people, sick children, preparing meals, laundry, house projects, and countless deadlines. Your work day is hectic. However, the sleep warrior's "day" begins when he lays down at night. We should begin our "day" by lying down at night at 9:00 or 10:00 o'clock and getting eight hours of sleep. When we get eight hours of sleep, we improve our immune system and cognition, have more energy, feel better, help prevent cancer, reduce stress, delay premature aging, facilitate self-care, etc. A good night's sleep is foundational to self-care.

I: Improvement

There is a famous Zen saying, "You are perfect as you are but there is room for improvement." If we start each day with this frame of mind, we are accepting ourselves for what we are: human. As humans, we live with the paradox of a perfect soul inside an imperfect body. When we constantly seek self-improvement, we maintain a beginners mind. With a beginners mind one remains eager for learning, open to infinite possibilities, and open to improvement. Perhaps we cannot obtain some kind of mythical perfection. But we can always strive for improvement. When we strive for improvement, we enjoy the journey. The destination of great health will come once we focus on daily improvement and enjoying the journey.

O: One person always comes first: Yourself

Think of life as a journey with a thousand steps. The first step should be taking great care of yourself. Once we have taken care of ourselves, we have the energy and resources to care for others. Making self-care your first priority is not narcissism or weakness. On the contrary, it takes discipline and courage and is the most powerful first step one should take. Imagine if your mind and body are ravaged by disease from years of self-neglect and abuse with drugs, alcohol and junk food. How effective is such a person in helping others? Now imagine if through self-care you have fostered a strong and healthy mind and body. Which body temple do you want to have as a vehicle for helping others?

N: Nourish your body and mind daily

Every day, carve out time for exercise and for planning healthy meals. Every day create sacred time for reading uplifting inspirational literature that feeds the soul. With the proper diet and exercise plan you are nourishing your body. With daily time created for music, art, meditation, inspirational literature you are nourishing the mind and soul.

When you practice self-compassion, you live a life in balance. With balance and moderation you engender a special energy that allows you to become a healthy vehicle for helping others. With self-compassion, we are better able to be of service to humanity.

Conclusion

THERE IS SO MUCH HATRED, VIOLENCE, NEGATIVITY, bigotry, Islamophobia, homophobia, sexism, discrimination, and fear mongering in today's world that we need a strong antidote. We cannot combat this negativity with more negativity. The answer is combating hate with love.

There are five universal principles with deep roots in Vedanta, Ayurveda, and Yoga going back thousands of years. In the 1800's, Charles and Myrtle Fillmore, philosophers of the New Thought movement, developed the Five Unity Principles as the foundation of their new church. I have given the five principles a secular interpretation through the lens of modern day science and recent discoveries in medicine.

Practicing these principles immediately engenders numerous health benefits. Modern science has revealed the secrets to avoid premature aging, prevent and reverse chronic diseases, promote abiding joy and happiness, and support exceptional longevity. They can be practiced by anyone regardless of age, race, religion or gender. The simple mnemonic device, L.O.V.E.S. reminds us of the practice.

Live Your Truth: Knowledge is Not Enough

Life's purpose (dharma) and meaning is found through practicing what you preach. Walking the walk promotes health by delaying biological aging. Not only will you look younger physically, but you also positively affect the aging process at the genetic level. When you live your truth, you develop an imperturbable mind. This leads to complete self-control and inner freedom. By living your truth you spontaneously gain profound equanimity (Sama) and reduce stress. When you live your truth you directly combat the five poisons that lead to bondage. The five poisons are ignorance, egoism, attachment, hatred, and fear of death. The remedy which is attained by living your truth, is wisdom through self-knowledge, defenselessness by not taking anything personally, inner detachment, love, and fearlessness. Practicing this principle alone will bring about a profound inner and outer transformation in your life!

One Presence and One Power: Interconnectedness Of the Cosmos

Modern science has discovered that we are all interconnected. Through the dialectic process of inquiry (Vichara) we look deeply into ahimsa and nonviolence. This lifestyle engenders nonviolence in thought, word and deed. We discover the best nutrition plan for the human body by honoring ahimsa and the precautionary principle.

Validation Through All Natural Medication: Meditation

There are over 100 billion neurons in the human brain with over 100 trillion connections. Through meditation we promote a healthy brain and engender neurogenesis. Through the practice of meditation, one can decrease stress hormones, reduce anxiety, decrease inflammation, increase neuroplasticity, improve the immune system, and slow the aging process. When you practice meditation and mindfulness, you promote serenity (manah prasada). Serenity is the quality of living with profound peace of mind, and complete fulfillment. With serenity, there is no external situation that could disturb your inner peace.

Experience is Created by Thoughts: Power of Positive Psychology

Modern psychology has proven that we create our own happiness through the power of our thoughts. Scientists have revealed that mindfulness of the present moment brings happiness. Also, one can synthesize their own happiness, no matter the external circumstances. Mindfulness allows one to live in the present moment thereby increasing not only happiness, but also contentment (Santosha). Contentment is the deep satisfaction with one's situation in life.

Stardust In Everyone:
Power Of Social Networks

The human body is composed of a billion billion billion atoms. An astonishing 93% of this mass is stardust! Since we're all so intricately connected with one another and the cosmos, we should live in harmony. Namaste means "the light within me honors the light within you." We connect at a deeper level when we recognize the miracle in all beings. This connection with others forms special bonds, a social network. Good associations (satsang) have powerful healing benefits. Modern scientific literature shows that strong social networks promote longevity. There is so much hate, fear and violence in today's world. This final principle is a direct remembrance, an antidote, to this hatred by revealing the power of namaste.

Imagine if everyone in our world lived the Five Universal Principles. When we live our truth, recognize one presence and one power that connects us all, practice mindfulness and meditation, transform reality through the power of thought, and honor the sacredness of all life on earth, we create health, happiness and peace.

Live Your Truth

One Presence and
One Power

Validation Through Meditation

Experience is Created
By Thoughts

Stardust in Everyone

About the Author

AFTER SERVING IN THE UNITED STATES NAVY during the Iraq War, Dr. Gutierrez completed training as a Family Medicine Physician at the renowned Mayo Clinic. During residency, he presented original research on exceptional longevity.

From a blue collar, immigrant background, he is the first in his family to attend college and truly enjoys connecting with people from all walks of life. He came to America on the Mariel Boat lift as a four-year-old. As a refugee, he overcame enormous obstacles in search of the American dream. He was raised in the inner city of Miami by a single mother, with English as his second language. He was given the opportunity in this great country to pursue his dreams. He is a successful business owner of Gutierrez Holistic Family Medicine, LLC, and author of *Three Steps to Superior Health, An Evidence-Based Guide for Stress Reduction, Longevity, and Weight Loss* (Luminare Press, 2015).

His undergraduate degree in 1999, is Magna Cum Laude with a double major in Philosophy and Biology from Florida International University. He has studied advanced Integral yoga at the Yoga Research Foundation. Since 1998, Dr. Gutierrez has practiced daily meditation and has followed a whole-foods plant-based diet for optimal health.

Dr. Gutierrez graduated from the Philadelphia College of Osteopathic Medicine in 2003 with honors. While studying osteopathic medicine, he instructed a weekly yoga class for students, faculty, and staff.

Dr. Gutierrez is President-Elect of Osteopathic Physicians and Surgeons of Oregon. He is passionate about teaching and is Clinical Assistant Professor of Family Medicine at Western University and Pacific Northwest University. He is also the Oregon Regional Assistant Dean for Pacific Northwest University Medical School. Orestes shares a holistic lifestyle with his wife, Pamela, their three children, and two dogs.